Dancing In The Bird Bath

by Gayle Dyer with Walter Jenkins

Introduction

"Hope is the thing with feathers that perches in the soul." Emily Dickinson.

Many people have told me I should write a book about my life. I resisted this for a long time and wondered, "Do I have a story worth telling?"

It finally became clear to me I am called to put my story in print. I no longer have a choice as to whether or not I share my journey with you. I hope you understand it is not me, but our Father above, who puts the words on these pages.

Words are very powerful things. God created the entire universe using only the spoken word.

I look back at the events in my life and see God's presence at every stage. It wasn't always easy, but, even when things were the darkest, I leaned on God, put one foot in front of the other, and kept moving.

I have come to understand every trial I endured was a blessing. It would have been easy to give up when I was going through these challenging times. But that is not how I choose to live. By embracing the things that happened to me, the good and the bad, my joy and peace overflow.

Some of you will face challenges that seem too large to overcome. You may feel your life is over and there is no hope. These moments are not stop signs on the road of life. They only mark the end of one stage and the beginning of another.

I would never wish any of the challenges I faced on anyone else, and I would never have chosen for them to happen. But I also know I would not have the joy and success I have today if I had not travelled the path that was laid before me.

I have tried to live my life with a servant's attitude. When I think about what makes me truly happy and content, it is almost always when I have been able to do something for those around me.

This attitude came from my family. I remember a time when my grandfather was ill and lived with my parents. Watching my mother care for him during those times taught me about the gifts of mercy and service. I also learned how to find humor and to feel content even in the most difficult of times. So it's natural that I would try to use my life to help others.

I am writing this book to answer to the question, "How can I serve you?" I hope the stories in this book shine like silver boxes tied with colored ribbons, that you unwrap each of them with excitement, and that they warm your heart and lift your spirits.

I pray that my story helps you experience the peace of God's presence and teaches you to "live in the now," like a bird in the air. Savor each day and relish the joy, laughter, and even the sadness that is given to you. Every once in a while, maybe when your life seems the darkest, take your shoes off, laugh like nobody is watching, and dance in a bird bath.

There were times that I wondered if I was doing the right thing by writing this book. I look out my window and see a gorgeous robin frolic in the birdbath in the backyard and can't help but laugh.

Harold, Ludia, Gayle and Harvey Yoakum.

The Nest

I grew up during simpler times. When I think about what my children and grandchildren have faced, I know I was blessed to have grown up when things were not as complicated as they are now.

I spent my childhood with both of my parents, Harold and Ludia Yoakum, and my younger brother, Harvey, in a small house on the south side of Oklahoma City. I always referred to our house as a cottage. Not that there was anything quaint about it, but it was the smallest house on the block. I loved to read as a child, and in all of my storybooks the characters lived in wonderful little "cottages" deep in the woods. That is how I saw my life.

Books have always been a powerful influence in my life. I

remember when I learned to read. I was looking at the Sunday funny papers when the words just started making sense. I felt elated as the words came together and I saw them in my head. I still have the "Dick and Jane" reader my brother and I used in school.

That was before television, and radio was our entertainment. One day, my brother found an injured bird needing our help. Harvey has always been tenderhearted and compassionate. He found a box, put the bird in it, and left it on the radio overnight. Our radio, like most of them back then, didn't just sit on a shelf. It sat on a library table. In my mind, it was a big piece of furniture and the entire living room was laid out in front of it. The radio was our entertainment. It had vacuum tubes, and the radio would warm up and radiate heat.

The bird got warm during the night, and this caused one small problem. It had mites, and they jumped off and spread throughout the house. Mom laughs about it now, but that morning she turned the entire house upside down to get rid of all the bugs that escaped from the bird's wings.

I don't remember fighting with Harvey when we were children. He once got angry with me when I wrecked his bicycle, but I can't remember any other times we weren't happy. Of course, there was the time he flushed all of my kitchen toys down the commode.

Our parents had to call a plumber to fix the problem, but I don't count that time because my parents were probably madder than I was.

My Daddy worked at Wilson Company, a meat packing plant, for his entire career, and my grandfather and several of my uncles worked with him. Sometimes, when Daddy wanted to get ahead, he would work a second job at night. No wonder my work ethic has always been so strong. I grew up watching my father working hard and being loyal to the same company for years and wondered, "Doesn't everybody do that?"

He was always a very gracious man. I remember trying out a new recipe for cupcakes when I was a girl. The recipe called for "whole eggs." I took those words literally and put the whole eggs into the bowl, shell and all. Daddy ate a cupcake and never batted an eye. He even told me he liked the "extra crunch."

Dad loved people and was a story teller. He loved doing the grocery shopping and would get a list from Mom so he would know what to bring home.

His clothes were always impeccable, and he never left the house without his hat and cowboy boots. Regardless of where he was going, he had to smell nice.

He had a ritual he would have to do each night before he went to bed. He walked throughout the house, fluffed all the pillows on the couch, and made sure all the doors and windows were locked. Mom would always laugh about this.

My dad was always meticulously groomed. He took his time, and enjoyed it, but you would never know he had done it if you followed behind him in the bathroom. He was always careful to clean up after himself.

When Dad bought new boots, he would smell them. He loved the smell of new leather. And he enjoyed getting his boots shined. It was a thrill for him to sit in the chair and chat with the men who buffed and polished his boots.

My mother was a great homemaker, like all the women of her generation. They were the inspiration for Harriet Nelson, and our home was picture-perfect clean.

When my brother and I came home from school, we were greeted by the smell of baked bread and Stanley furniture polish. Stanley products were like Tupperware or Pampered Chef. Women would have parties and sell them to one another.

Mom was the queen of her cottage and knew how to make it like she wanted. "Cleanliness is next to godliness," she would tell me. "A little soap and water goes a long way."

She also used to say, "You can always make things better than they are." With a little effort, you can always polish yourself or your surroundings. My youngest daughter, Beth, might say I take this lesson a little too far. She says I can take a burlap sack and turn it into something fantastic.

Those were only a few of the words I heard my mother say when I was a child. Children are like sponges, and they quickly absorb whatever environment they are exposed to. Words can stick in a child's head. If you feed them positive words and examples, they will grow into positive, happy people. Most of the examples I saw as a child taught me to be happy, healthy, content, and loving, and this was a blessing.

Happiness is a choice, and I was always a happy child. I remember once when my mother and I were in the store. We walked down an aisle holding hands.

A stranger came up to us and smiled. "What a happy child you have," she told my mother. My mother thanked her and said, "Yes she is a happy child. She is happy all the time." As my mother spoke, she squeezed my hand. As a child, I took it as a cue I was expected to always be happy.

As I grew older, I understood there were times when it was okay to not be happy. It is normal to be sad as you make your way through the challenges life presents you. But you don't want to dwell on these times. You have to remember the joyous times and all the blessings you have. I tried to teach my children it is okay to have feelings, but you can't turn this into a destructive thing. You don't want to let the darkness overtake you. Accept the pain, learn from it, and always be grateful for the good times.

I'm glad I came to accept people won't be happy all the time. That would be crazy. There are times when you won't feel well, and it's honest to admit when you aren't happy. You have to be honest about your emotions, and it is also important to handle them with grace.

Mother loved doing housework. After she would iron our curtains, she would hang them back up, and I would watch them flutter in the wind as it blew through the open window. Our clothes were hung to dry on the line in the backyard.

Once, during the sweltering heat of an Oklahoma summer, my brother and I could not resist the temptation of the cool laundry blowing in the breeze. He and I wrapped the clean sheets around our sweaty bodies and cooled ourselves. The Queen was not happy with us.

My brother, like all little boys, was prone to his share of mischievousness. There was a little neighborhood store two blocks from our home. All the families in the neighborhood could charge their groceries and pay the bill at the end of the month. One day when he was four or five years old, my brother wandered off to the store and came back with a little brown sack. Our Mom asked what was in the sack, and my brother told her it was candy and caps for his toy gun.

She asked him how he paid for these things. He looked her straight in the eyes and said, "Charge it to my daddy." Mother promptly marched him back to the store and made him return the things he had "bought."

Acee Blue Eagle Glasses.

Treasures

In those days, many of the stores we frequented gave out dishes and place settings as promotions. My father would fill the car with gas at Kerr-McGee, and our family eventually had a full set of Acee Blue Eagle glasses and pitcher on a wooden serving tray. These beautiful frosted white glasses had vibrant Native American images painted on them. Mother loved these, and to this day they sit on the counter in my kitchen. We see them every day, and they continue to bring joy to me and my family.

My parents' set of Revere wear was bought with S&H green stamps. In fact, all of our glassware and crystal came from S&H. That was a real thrill as a kid. Whenever we went to the store, after the clerk rang up our total, he would reach up to a big machine that sat on a metal pole next to the register. He would turn a dial, and it would spit out green stamps we would lick and stick in little booklets. The more you spent at the store the more stamps you would get, and the quicker the booklets would fill up. When you had enough stamps, you would take the booklets to the S&H store and redeem them. It was so exciting for us to paste the stamps in the booklets and plan what we would buy when it they were full.

There was another set of dishes my uncle had given to my mom. Over the years, they would get chipped or break. I developed a ritual. Every year, on the Monday after our company holds its show in Tulsa, I would stay for an extra day and stroll through the antique shops in Jenks, a suburb of Tulsa known for its wonderful stores. On one of these excursions, I found a platter with the same pattern my mother had. I instantly loved it because it brought back so many wonderful memories.

Like my mother, I have always treasured certain items. They are only material things, and it is not the material that means so much to me. It is the love, affection, and reminder of family I think of when I see these things. I have a creamer and sugar bowl from my father's childhood. The painted blue birds flying around the outside of these remind me to have faith. God will take care of my needs, and I shouldn't worry.

I have the apron my great-grandmother made for me when I was a little girl. When I look at it, I can smell the sugar cookies we baked in her kitchen. I was so blessed to be part of a family that took the time to nurture me and instill the values that help make me who I am today. I wish she were here so I could cut the cookies out of the dough one more time.

There was a time when my dad's parents moved into the house behind ours. I used to gather eggs from their chicken coop. My grandmother would crush the eggshells and put them in the chickenfeed. I didn't know it at the time, but I have since learned this is good for the chickens and acts like a vitamin.

In the corner of my dining room sits a wood burning cook stove that belonged to my first husband's father. I don't know how anyone could have used it. If my family were depending on me to cook with that stove, we would all have starved to death or acquired a taste for burnt food.

Photographs have also meant a lot to us, and many of the walls in my home are lined with pictures that document our lives. A photographer used to come through my childhood neighborhood with a pony, and we would have our picture taken on it. I never realized how important horses were to us, but as I look at the pictures that line these walls, I see all of us sitting on horses at one time or another. We have a beautiful picture of my mother in the saddle.

Ermon, my third husband, and I even went to a ranch in Brush Creek, Wyoming, after we were married. We shared the weekend with Harvey, his wife, and my mother and enjoyed the chuck wagon, the campfire, and riding the horses.

Gayle And Harvey's Picture Perfect Pony.

Harvey, Ludia, Harold and Gayle Yoakum.

Family

I value family so much because I grew up with such a loving, fun family. We would often visit my mother's parents in the summertime.

My grandfather plowed his fields with mules. I used to take him cold water in a jar, which was a welcome relief during the sweltering afternoons of the Oklahoma summer. I had to walk through a patch of blackberries to reach him, and I would always grab a handful on the way back.

They had a wonderful garden. We would sit on the ground, pluck tomatoes off the vine, slice and salt them, and eat them right there.

They lived out in the country and had no running water. There were rain barrels to collect the water as it fell from the sky. One of the barrels sat next to the porch, and my brother had to see what was inside it. He stood on his tippy toes, peered over the lid of the barrel, and fell in. Fortunately, our aunt was there and grabbed him before he could get hurt.

That story tells a lot about my brother. He has always been more adventurous than I have. I always admired him for his adventurous streak. He knew everybody for blocks around and would investigate anything. I was much more of a straight arrow.

My grandparents also had a cellar, which was cool and damp. I never knew it, but they used to make elderberry wine and keep it down there. My mother told me she went in the cellar and had a private wine sampling at a young age. Suffice it to say, she became a teetotaler early on.

Gayle Yoakum's Senior Picture.

Work

I learned about work and commitment while I was fairly young. I began babysitting for neighbors at the age of twelve. By the time I was thirteen, I wanted a "real" job.

During my junior high and high school years, my family lived in Del City, Oklahoma, a small suburb east of Oklahoma City. My parents were friends with our local druggist, Harold Thompson, who owned and operated Thompson Drug. He became my first mentor outside of school and church.

I feel I was always mature for my age. The summer I turned thirteen, I began working for Harold at the drugstore. That was a big deal for me. I had my first real job that came with a paycheck.

Harold hired me to make drinks, shakes, and banana splits behind the soda fountain at his drug store. Every day for lunch, some of the most important people in town would come by and I would get to serve them. I kept my ears open and listened to the owner and my "soda fountain friends."

It didn't take me very long to know what I wanted to do with my earnings. My parents always provided nicely for Harvey and me to have the things we needed for school, so any extra money I earned I could spend on myself.

I quickly realized if I saved my money until the end of August, I could go on the greatest and most fun shopping spree a girl could ask for. I could buy several pairs of "fun" shoes, handbags to match, and all the little accessorizing items.

As the summers passed, I continued working at the drugstore and even began helping out in the cosmetic and gift areas. I was always listening to and watching Harold. He coached me well on "serving" the customer. One of the phrases that stayed in my mind was, "The sweetest sound in a customer's ear is their own name."

Many of the local business men and political leaders would take coffee breaks or spend lunch time there. I became acquainted with them as I served them. I gained knowledge listening to their conversations concerning business, politics, religion, money matters, and so forth.

Some days my Mom would bring me a plate lunch. Harold would almost always ask me what she brought and offer to trade me for something from behind the counter. He loved Mother's cooking.

I didn't know it yet, but I was already tuned into how much I liked business. I quickly learned how to handle people. I also learned a lot about myself, including how important it was I earn the respect of the people I worked for.

I grew respect for the way men think. I was impressed with the way they were so direct when dealing with problems. If there is an issue between them, they address it and get it over with. Women can be game players and dance around the real issue before they find a solution.

Men also handle their emotions better. Emotions can get in the way and keep us from being the people God wants us to be.

In a small way, I was in summer school. I was learning from peers in my own community who were respected leaders.

My brother Harvey started a small lawn business during those summer days. He also worked for a restaurant and a grocery store.

There are times I have thought of myself as a workaholic. As I write down my memories for you to read, I am learning more about myself and know this term does not apply to me. I treasure my work and want to use the talents God has given me to the best of my ability.

The lessons I learned behind that soda counter were worth more than any ten classes I could have taken in business school. The relationships I forged with those people enhanced my life and will always be of great value to me.

There is an old saying, "When the student is ready, the teacher will appear." I think of that and am reminded to always have an attitude that says, "I am ready!" I also think of how much I have to learn, and how little time I have to learn it in.

Wayne's Mission Birdhouse.

Faith

Memories of church, Sunday school, and Bible school are some of the most cherished experiences of my life. Those were times of much joy. Lessons were learned, and fun times were shared. My Sunday school teacher, Mrs. Dunlap, holds a special place in my heart. Because of her love and prayers I became a child of God at the tender age of nine.

I loved summer Bible school and could concentrate one year's worth of work into a single week. I especially loved the arts and crafts lessons we had, and I remember making a bird cage out of yarn and soda straw. After I put it together and decorated it, I was thrilled at the sight.

The lessons that really stand out in my mind came from my parents, teachers at school, and Mrs. Dunlap at church. I learned how much God loved me, to love and respect God and others, and to glorify Him with my life.

I was also taught about contentment, but did not fully grasp the lesson at that time. As I grew in knowledge, the understanding followed. In Philippians 4:12, the Bible says, "I know how to live on almost nothing or with everything. I have learned the secret of living in every situation." This is something I try to apply every day.

I have always felt close to the Lord. There is one thing I have shared with only a few people because it sounds so goofy. When I was nine, I had my tonsils removed. This was such an overpowering experience for me, I close my eyes and can still see the operating room behind the walls of the small brick hospital. As the anesthesiologist put me under (back then they used ether), he and a nun wearing a full habit were standing next to me. I saw a large green "Z" at the end of a tunnel and a smaller "Z" leaving my head. I heard a voice say, "Come, my son." As a child, it was very comforting and made me feel like God was there taking care of me.

I have come to recognize this as the Alpha and the Omega. This vision has been in my mind ever since.

I have never forgotten this event, but never told anyone because I didn't know how they would react. There are other moments I felt God reveling Himself to me.

I have always considered myself sensitive, both to matters of the spirit and to the feelings of others. Drawing closer to God makes these experiences possible.

Another special moment happened shortly after Roy, my first husband, died. I was visiting my brother and his family at their home. Harvey and his family have some beautiful land with a lake on it. Looking at the water is very comforting for me, and I stood there one special day looking across to the shore on the other side. As I thought about my life, I saw Roy standing on the other side of the lake. I know what I saw, and no one will ever convince me otherwise. This was God's way of letting me know Roy was in his hands, and that he was on the other side.

We spent the first Christmas without Roy at my parents' place. I went there several times after he died. My family has always given me such strength and hope when I needed it. It takes an hour to drive there, and I always called this my "windshield time." Once I got to their house, I sat by the Christmas tree as the children were laughing.

I felt a sudden warmth, as if something were coming from the lights hanging on the tree. This was very intense and comforting and filled my heart with joy.

My mother was by my side, and knew something had happened. I told her how peaceful I felt. "God just gave me my Christmas present," I told her. The warmth I felt was God using His grace to let me know He is always with me. If you are sensitive to what God is doing in your life, perhaps you will have moments like these.

God has always made the holidays comforting for me. Whenever you lose a loved one, holidays can be difficult. They are a time when we treasure our families, and this can intensify our feeling of loss. But they can also be a time for you to collect all your joyous memories and wrap them around you like a blanket.

Gayle In Front Of Her Grade School (Lafayette) At S.W. 44th.

Humor

I enjoy revisiting the memories of my childhood. Life was simple and innocent. My parents provided a safe and happy home for my brother and me. I remember so vividly our small, cottage-like house. The grass was well-kept and flowers blossomed around the porch. During spring and summer we would run barefoot through the cool, green grass.

We used our imaginations playing outdoors. There was no TV, no cell phones, no video games, or any of the electronic "necessities" we have today.

We listened to our favorite programs on the radio. I can close my eyes and see my mother ironing the laundry while she listened to her "soap shows."

We did not know the term "stay at home mom." Mother was expected to be the queen of the cottage, just like Dad was expected to be the loving provider and leader of our little family. He and Mom worked tirelessly to maintain the outside and inside of our home.

They knew how to add fun and humor to our lives. There were always family picnics, outings, trips to the amusement park, and sharing homemade, hand-cranked ice cream with neighbors. It was not unusual to see Mother and her family playing leapfrog during family reunions.

Fun is still very important to my brother and me. When I hear about something I want to do, I might say, "That sounds like a fun thing to do." Harvey puts it a little stronger. One of his favorite expressions is, "We are going to have a very large time."

My mother will do anything for a laugh. Several years ago, she decided to replace the commode in one of the bathrooms of her house. It wasn't broken, she just wanted to make a change. Instead of throwing it away, she sold it at a garage sale. When people came to the house for the sale, they would see the toilet sitting in her driveway. Mother saw these people walking by, and before too long she got a newspaper and sat on the toilet. When people would look at her she would lower the paper and smile. It was so funny my daughters took a picture and posted it online.

We lived two blocks from our grade school. Walking to school during the fall was my absolute favorite time. The beauty of all the vibrant colored leaves that swirled all over the street invited me to run through them. The excitement of seeing, hearing, smelling, and experiencing God's handiwork was exhilarating.

Southern Hills Baptist Church Where Gayle Is A Member.

Seasons

I stand in awe of the change in every season. The way God uses His paintbrush in nature is astonishing. When we allow Him to take the canvas of our lives He can produce beautiful masterpieces. Some are highly detailed miniatures, while others are grand and sweeping, epic in size. Some of our canvasses are filled with stormy, dark clouds, but by the stroke of His brush, the canvas can be filled with sunlight, blue sky, and a sense of His peace and grace.

Through the many dark and cloudy times in my life, God's love has added warmth, bright colors, and joy to my canvas with the gentle stroke of His paintbrush.

I have wonderful memories from my years in grade school.

The teachers were so neatly dressed, used white handkerchiefs, wore lovely set hair, and, of course, wore fragrant perfume. The love and respect I had for my teachers was immense. I watched everything they did and said.

It is so important for each and every one of us to be aware of how we speak to children during their early years. In Proverbs 16:24, God tells us, "Pleasant words are a honeycomb to the soul." The words we hear as children can follow us into adulthood. Use encouraging words, a loving tone of voice, and, when you have to, correct your children gently. These are seeds that will not grow until they become adults.

My mother had an "Avon lady" who sold her creams, makeup, and perfume. I always looked forward to the day she made deliveries. Then I could try out the latest fragrance Mom had ordered and smell just like my teachers.

Even when I was too young to say it properly, I always asked Mom if I could wear her perfume. She let me put on a dab of "smelly" when she put some on herself.

I have always been a very tactile person. I appreciate textures, sights, sounds, and smells. I thank God for these gifts as they add such richness to our lives and souls.

When we were children growing up, I adored my "little brother" Harvey. From the day he was born he had an adventuresome spirit, a curious mind, and the ability to charm everyone.

In our adult lives, as often happens in families, our relationship went through a time of brokenness, due to immaturity and a lack of knowledge on how to deal with the challenges we face in relationships. As the years passed, God healed hearts and mended broken spirits. As the scripture tells us, "He will give back the years the locusts have taken away."

Today, the deep love and admiration we have for one another is once again strong. Only God can reconcile people and make relationships better than before. Thank you, God, for bringing my brother back into my life.

Snow And Gayle.

Friendship

The cherished friendships we make in childhood teach us to relate to one another. We learn as we mature that different friends have different purposes in our lives. It is God's way of giving us people who can help us through the different seasons and situations we experience. Some are for the moment, others are for a lifetime.

We can write a list of many, many significant people who have touched our lives over the years. What I have learned from these people could fill a book.

We have other relationships where people come into our lives for a brief time, but then we forget the exact connection with that person. If we are fortunate, at some point those people reappear in our lives and we are blessed by the re-connection. It can be a moment of warmth and tenderness of heart.

They can relate to a moment when you said something to someone kind to them or showed them an act of mercy. It is so very important to let our words and actions toward others demonstrate an attitude of "lifting up" a person. It is a great blessing to be the "wind beneath" someone's wings.

"The glory of friendship is not the outstretched hand, nor the kindly smile nor the joy of companionship; it is the spiritual inspiration that comes to one when he discovers that someone else believes in him and is willing to trust him." Ralph Waldo Emerson.

The gift of friendship is a treasure indeed and has given me a life of precious memories. From childhood until the present day, I have always placed great value on lasting friendships.

When there is a distance or gap in time between visits and chats, one's heart quickens and laughter abounds in your soul when your paths cross again. True friendship never goes away in our hearts.

God created men and women to have the need for friendship. We are created in God's own image. Adam was created by God for the purpose of giving God someone to communicate with, as well as to be the caretaker of all of His magnificent creations.

I often give speeches and always take the time to include one of my favorite poems. It was written by Sam Walter Foss and speaks to my heart as to how we should treat those we have the privilege of meeting as we travel the roads of our lives.

The House by the Side of the Road

There are hermit souls that live withdrawn
In the peace of their self-content;
There are souls, like stars, that swell apart,
In a fellowless firmament;
There are pioneer souls that blaze their paths
Where highways never ran;
But let me live by the side of the road
And be a friend to man.

Let me live in a house by the side of the road,
Where the race of men go by;
The men who are good and the men who are bad,
As good and as bad as I.
I would not sit in the scorner's seat,
Or hurl the cynic's ban;
Let me live in a house by the side of the road
And be a friend to man.

I see from my house by the side of the road,
By the side of the highway of life,
The men who press with the ardor of hope,

The men who are faint with the strife.
But I turn not away from their smiles nor their tears
Both parts of an infinite plan;
Let me live in my house by the side of the road
And be a friend to man.

Let me live in my house by the side of the road
Where the race of men go by;
They are good, they are bad, they are weak,
They are strong,
Wise, foolish - so am I.
Then why should I sit in the scorner's seat
Or hurl the cynic's ban?
Let me live in my house by the side of the road
And be a friend to man.

Ludia's Perspective...At Her 90th Birthday Party.

Perspective

As I write these words in 2010, there are several important events happening in my life. One of them is the fact that I celebrated my seventy-first birthday. What a journey the years have been. My birthday falls around Mother's Day each year. Our family always gets together to rejoice on this holiday, and my birthday comes along for a free ride.

I am so very blessed this year to have my mother and my two daughters with me to share this special time. The relationship between a mother and daughter is a special gift. From birth, through childhood, and into maturity, the bond develops a fullness and adds a joy to our lives that is better demonstrated than described.

As we nurture our children, the miracle of love and trust blossoms in our hearts. We become best friends to one another. These treasured relationships help us through the difficulties we face in life.

When my daughters were born, I remember wanting to hold them close and protect them. God holds us in the shadow of His wings, the birds of the air protect their young, and we naturally want to safeguard our children. I stand in awe at this beautiful, protective, and nurturing spirit God has placed within females, not only within humans, but to all the creatures in God's kingdom.

There were times of struggle, conflict, doubt, and fear as my daughters grew into teenagers. During these challenges, I relied heavily on the Lord to help guide and lead me as a parent. As you know, children do not come with roadmaps or instruction manuals. Raising children definitely keeps you humble and dependant on God's guidance.

The death of their father intensified the stress and fear of raising children. The three of us each had our individual grief to process. I tried to be a mother and father to each of the girls. The Lord revealed to me I could not be both. As these hard and difficult times have passed, I am so very thankful for the loving and trustful relationship that has carried us to the place we are now.

Both of the girls are now mothers. They understand more than ever the gifts, duties, joys, and heartbreak motherhood brings. When the girls share with me their challenges and their difficult situations, I think back to our trials and tribulations. Rather than saying, "I told you so," I offer them a warm and loving smile and words of encouragement. This leaves each of us with feelings of hope and the promise everything will be okay.

My relationship with my mother has undergone a complete role reversal. She is in the winter of her life, and I am in the autumn of mine. The experiences we have shared, the tears we have shed, and the laughs that have filled our days make our lives a remarkable adventure.

For the sacrifices, love, and trust she gave to me, it is now my privilege to return these gifts to her. When we serve one another from birth to eternity, we are demonstrating true love.

June 23, 2010, brought me many happy memories. Fifty-three years ago I was married to my first husband, Roy, the father of my two daughters. I celebrated the day by wearing a pendant he had made for me.

I began to reflect on my "journey of three lifetimes." I have been blessed with three marriages, each one was different yet they were all the same. These three special men have added much joy to my life.

Until now, I have not given much thought to the fact I still have all three of the dresses I wore in each of my weddings. I felt the need to go to the closet where I keep them. I had never asked myself this question before, but I suddenly wondered, "Why had I so lovingly put these away?" As I unwrapped them, I sat down with the dresses around me. The tears flowed gently as I read the wonderful story these garments told. I felt the fabrics, noticing the difference in the styles of each dress, the colors, and the trim. The first one was pale, ivory white with tiny buttons, the second was soft beige with lovely crochet trim, and the third was a sophisticated taupe with elegant beadwork.

These dresses tell the stories of three different seasons of my life, spring, summer and fall. All three are similar, yet so different. They represent a total of forty-three years of marriage to three vastly different, but equally loving, caring, and wonderful men.

I have been asked, "How can you love again after being in love with and devoted to a person for so many years?" The answer is simple. When you allow God to bring you the person He selects, your heart and mind will open, and you will be able to give and receive the love you deserve.

As I enter the winter years of my life I treasure the memoires of the beautiful times, the challenging times, and the blessings of seasons past. I look forward to the journey ahead. Loving and being loved are two of the greatest gifts we can receive.

Roy And Gayle's Senior Prom 1957.

Roy

I am privileged to share my story with you. It is not easy for me to speak or write about myself. I did not do this for my own glory or to make myself famous. Our paths have crossed because God has given me a story to tell, one I believe can help you as you move through the stages and challenges of your life.

Everyone will experience grief and loss. It is as natural and inevitable as the sun rising in the east and setting in the west. When you face the loss of someone or something you love, you don't have to accept it at face value. Look beyond the pain and find joy in the memories.

There are so many losses we experience in life that make us

familiar with grief. Sometimes, it seems like sadness is all we know.

These losses can include the deaths of husbands, wives, parents, grandparents, children, or friends. They can also include the losses of relationships, pets, careers, health issues, and the list goes on.

We all handle the grief process differently and go through it at our own pace. God has created each of us to be unique, and we will move according to the strengths and weaknesses He has given us.

I have found a comfortable way to grieve, and I hope by sharing it, you can handle the challenges that come your way. Please understand there is no way to avoid loss or pain in this lifetime. What I am offering you is not a detour around painful times. Hopefully, my words will make the journey less painful and will help you see difficult times are not a stop sign at the end of the road. If you look at these times as moments of opportunity and faith, they can become the beginnings of new journeys that are joyful beyond anything you could have dreamed.

When I was growing up, I had the privilege of knowing many successful people in my town. I didn't know it at the time, but it was really a great business education for me.

That was probably a bit unusual for a teenage girl in those days. The emphasis for girls was not necessarily to do well in high school so they could be accepted into a good college or start a new career. Our goal was to get married after we got out of high school. This was how we were brought up at home. Girls were expected to take care of the nest (by cooking, cleaning, and caring for the children), and boys were expected to be the bread winners and bring home the bacon.

Even schools reinforced these roles. Girls took classes like home economics, art, and social skills. These were all designed to help us raise our families and manage our homes. That was our career. Even if a girl did go to college, she would generally come back as a teacher and teach the same subjects to a new generation of students.

I'm not complaining about this. When I graduated from high school, I wanted to be a wife and mother. I embraced both of these roles, and I am still proud and blessed to have been both. But I am glad to see the girls of today have more options than I did. I also know the limited roles I was allowed to fill as a child may have impacted me when I started my own business. I was never allowed to be part of a team like the boys were, and I know this hindered me when I became one of eight women who started their own company.

I was never a great student, and the truth is I was average. I am always impressed when I meet someone who has a high level of education. That shows so much discipline and drive. I have come to understand education alone is no guarantee of success in the business world. Regardless of how educated you are, you have to "put in your time" to make your company grow.

I haven't kept many things from my school days, but I do have one note from a teacher. She seemed to think I had trouble dealing with people and sent a note home saying, "Gayle doesn't work well with others." I think of this and laugh as I look at the business I have helped build over the last twenty-five years. The business has grown in no small part due to my ability to forge relationships and work well with those around me.

Gayle And Roy.

First Love

I met my first husband, Roy Bowling, when I was a senior in high school. I don't recall looking to meet anyone, it was just one of those things that was meant to happen.

In those days, we didn't have any malls, and we didn't watch television. A big Friday night for teenagers was to go to the movies and then to the drive-in for a burger and a shake. Our favorite place in downtown Oklahoma City was called Hollies. That's where you would find me and my friends every Friday night. Afterwards, we would drag Main Street, which meant we would drive our cars down the street, turn around, and then drive back. It may not seem like much to people today, but for us, it was heaven.

On October 27, 1956, we were driving up and down Main Street when a yellow Jaguar with four boys pulled up alongside us. It was in October, which is always a special time in Oklahoma. The summers here are long and hot, and the humidity covers you like an old, wet blanket. When the first hint of winter comes in the cool, crisp October air, it is a welcome relief.

A boy wearing a leather jacket stuck his head out of the window and asked me my name. I was feeling a little playful and told him, "My name is in the funny paper." My maiden name is Yoakum, and one of the most popular cartoons at the time was "Li'l Abner," which featured a character with the last name Yoakum.

The boy who asked the question was Roy, and did I ever underestimate his persistence. Somehow, he put two and two together and figured out my last name. Then, he rooted through the phonebook and found my grandfather's phone number. Roy had the courage to call my grandfather, tell him who he was, and sweet talk him into giving him my phone number. That story always reminds me of how innocent we were back then. My grandfather didn't worry about giving a complete stranger my phone number because he didn't have to worry. If this happened today, Roy and I would never have had the chance to meet.

I later found out the yellow Jaguar belonged to one of Roy's friends. Roy owned a hot rod Ford with leather interior.

When I got to see him outside of the car, Roy looked so macho with his loafers, rolled up jeans, and black leather jacket.

After Roy called me, it didn't take long for us to realize things "felt right." We were married the following June. Some people might think we rushed things and we didn't develop a friendship before marrying. But we grew together over the next twenty-eight years and enjoyed our time together. From the very first time I spoke to him, Roy made me feel safe and comfortable. He was a very pleasant gentleman, and everyone liked him. We always worked well as a team, and were able to take care of our house and our garden.

I had a great deal of respect for Roy. He was five years older than I was, and when we met, he already had a good job. When he and I married, I went from one safe and secure nest to another.

He was very gifted at math, and worked at a steel company helping design steel structures used in buildings. He only had a few hours of education past high school, but was very good at his job. He worked for the same company for many years, and eventually opened the same type of business for himself.

Roy wanted a family, and was an incredible family man.

Much of this came from what he had endured as a child. When he was twelve, Roy's parents went through a terrible divorce. Divorce is never good. It destroys everyone who comes near it. Today, almost everyone knows someone whose family has been impacted by the end of a marriage. But when Roy was young, it was unusual for people to get divorced, and this made it even harder on him.

During the course of the divorce, Roy's parents argued over where he should live. Both parents wanted custody of him. Roy was eventually forced to stand in front of the judge and testify as to where he wanted to go. I can't imagine how terrible that must have been for a twelve-year old boy. Sometimes I think about how scared he must have been standing before a judge at the courthouse, with both of his parents arguing the other was unfit. Every child loves his parents, and I know it broke Roy's heart to have gone through that.

Some people would have had their hearts hardened by that and might become so cynical and scared they would never allow themselves to get close to anyone. But not Roy. He never forgot standing before the judge, and he swore that when he had a family, his children would never have to worry about their parents divorcing. His love of family had been tried by fire and made stronger. When married, he was totally committed to being the best husband and father he could be.

My children tell me how peaceful our home was. It was our safe place, and I am proud my daughters felt the comfort we wanted to give them. That is what home ought to be. Children should know both of their parents love and cherish them as gifts from God and will do everything they can to keep them safe and healthy. No child should ever think of home as a scary place or somewhere they are not wanted or loved.

Gayle And Roy...The Happy Couple.

The Goal

Roy and I were married shortly after I graduated from high school. We chose his birthday so he would never be able to forget our anniversary. I never lived alone, and I went from one safe and secure environment to another. I never had the chance to flap my wings and fly solo. That was "the goal," and once I was married, I thought that would be my life forever. I thought the two of us would grow old together just like my parents had. My job was to be a helpmate to my husband so he could be the provider. I had no idea that life wouldn't always be simple and carefree.

I believed Roy and I would have the "Ozzy and Harriet" life I thought my parents enjoyed. My parents made this look easy.

Dad worked at the same meatpacking plant for his entire career. Sometimes, he would even take a second job so he and my mother could have a little extra. My mother always kept my room for me, and I never concerned myself with housekeeping. She worried about every little detail, such as never letting any of the clothes in my closet touch. She wanted me to participate in all of the social things we had at school, like the pep club and glee club.

She may have done too good of a job. When I was married, I wasn't ready to keep a house. After Roy left for work in the morning, Mother would come over and teach me how to do things, like laundry and cleaning. She even had me ironing Roy's underwear and our tea towels. He must have thought he had the greatest deal ever, and we really had him buffaloed. Every day when he came home the house and everything in it looked perfect. Mom did the best she could to turn me into another Mrs. Cleaver, but I knew I couldn't keep that façade up for long.

Some men have trouble telling people they love them, but the men in my life have always told me how much they cared about me. When I was young, my father would pat my head, and tell me, "I love you whole bunches." I miss that so much. I was surrounded by people who made no secret of the fact I was loved. I grew up with my aunts and uncles encouraging me and telling me how much they cared about me. These are the words children need to hear.

Roy was great at giving presents, and this was one of the many ways I knew how much he loved me. Many times he would come home from work with a gift for me or the children. When I asked him what the occasions was, he would smile and say, "It's just because." We came to expect gifts on Tuesdays or Fridays. He rarely showed up without presents for us on those days, and he would always announce to us these were our Tuesday (or Friday) gifts. If we were in a store and one of us said she liked something, Roy would come back to the store later, buy it, and give it as a birthday or Christmas present. If you eyed it, you got it. His heart always led him to do sweet things like this, and everyone around him felt loved and appreciated.

He loved giving me cards and used these to tell me how much he cared for me. Every card he ever gave me was signed, "All my love, all my life."

We were once at an antiques show, and I saw several yards of handmade lace with an intricate heart pattern that was just beautiful. I looked at it for several moments and finally asked the clerk how much it cost.

"You don't want that," she said condescendingly. I looked at her, and I knew she thought I wouldn't be able to afford it.

I went outside the booth, and Roy asked me what happened. When I told him, he marched into the store and smiled at the woman. "The lady asked you the price of the lace. What is the price of the lace?" he asked.

When she told him, he told her to wrap the lace up and bought it on the spot. Roy was always very tactful, and he didn't say anything to hurt the woman, but he wanted to let the lady know she had embarrassed me. Before he left, he gave her one of my business cards to let her know I owned a store just like she did.

I was surprised when she came into my shop one day and apologized for how she had treated me. Not long after that she wrote me a nice letter. I still have the letter and lace.

I haven't forgotten the power of loving words. To this day, every time my brother and I talk we say, "I love you." I call my mother every night at 9:00 and tuck her in. If she is not feeling well, I go to her house to be by her side. I am so blessed to be able to give something back to her, and I will miss it when I don't have the opportunity to do it.

I learned this attitude from her. Seven years before I wrote these words, I watched my mother care for my father while he was dying. Mom still says the last day they spent together was the most beautiful time they ever had. They reminisced and got to relive so many of the special moments they had created. They went to bed together, like they had done so many times over the years. What a great memory to be left with.

When Mom woke up the next morning, Dad was in the same position he was in when he fell asleep. Mom woke up, read the paper, and made breakfast. As she tried to rouse him to the breakfast table, she realized he passed away during the night.

I couldn't begin to describe my grief after knowing Daddy had passed away. He had always been there for me, and I wished just one more time he could tell me how much he loved me. I loved him bunches, and I hope he knew that. I pray when the day comes for us to be reunited, he will pat my head and tell me he loves me.

As my mother sat weeping because her husband had gone to heaven without her, I knew we had to make some important decisions. My first two husbands had died before Daddy, and I knew we had to start planning for the service.

My mom sat in a chair, and I was at her feet patting her knee. "Mom, we have to think about arrangements," I said.

She held her head in her hands. "Oh honey, you take care of that. You have so much more experience than I do."

She paused for a moment and then looked at me. "I didn't mean that."

We both started laughing. She was right. I did have more experience burying husbands than she did. I had to use my pain and grief to help her. I had walked that road before and it was my privilege to ease her burden.

My Mom has shared stories of special moments she has experienced since Dad passed away. Sometimes she feels Dad's presence. Some people may think she is imagining these things. But I know she is not. I understand because I have these moments, too. There are times when something brushes up against me. The feeling is soft and gentle, and I like to think of angels' wings. Sometimes I feel it when I have to make a decision and I've prayed I make the right choice. My cat has flinched and looked at me at the same time. He cocks his little head as if he were watching something move across the room. I have studied that cat from the time he came into my life, and I know when something has his attention. Perhaps he also feels the soft touch of angels' wings.

Harvey And Gayle.

The West

Some people wonder how I can say I have truly loved all three of my husbands equally. They think if I committed my heart to one man I can never love anyone else. I don't look at it that way. Each one of the men I have known has given me something special. Roy offered me security and comfort, Wayne was spontaneous and fun, and Ermon is the supportive friend I will share the winter of my life with. God put these wonderful things together.

The truth is, I almost feel selfish. God has given me so many good years with the men in my life. I have always been loved so much. In some ways, it was almost too much. I have been blessed beyond belief to have lived the life I have been given.

I don't want you to think things were always perfect. We had our ups and downs. But we always found a way to work things out. Even through all the sadness we found a way to dance in the birdbath.

Roy and I eventually moved to Albuquerque, and this was a wonderful time of my life, although it was difficult for me at first. When we decided to move, I faced a great deal of anxiety. I turned to my faith and found comfort in any religious symbol I could find. As we drove to New Mexico, I looked at the telephone poles lining the road and thought of them as crosses. These signs from God gave strength and peace as we approached our new home.

I instantly fell in love with the southwest. The sky there is a special blue, and there is nothing else like it in the world. The air is always crisp and clear. I loved looking at the wide open vistas and the slow rolling brush. On some days you could stand outside and smell the sage that grew wild on the side of the road. At night, the aroma of piñion would waft in as people started fires in chimineas, the pear-shaped clay fireplaces found in every backyard.

Standing under the stars on a clear New Mexico night is magical. The sky lights up, as if there were a giant black tarp had been pricked so light from the hidden sun could find its way through.

Staring at God's handiwork is humbling and reminds me I am just one tiny grain of sand in His plan.

I suppose my love of the southwest goes back to my childhood. Back then, my brother Harvey and I loved going to the movies. Cowboy movies were popular, and there were three different theaters in our part of town. For a quarter, we could buy a ticket, and get a drink and popcorn. Harvey loved Hopalong Cassidy. My favorites were Roy Rogers and Dale Evans. Every week we would line up with many of the other kids in town and see how the good guys would beat the bad guys. Those movies instilled terrific mindset in kids. Good always triumphed, and the heroes acted with dignity and respect for each other, and even towards the villains. The good guys always wore white hats.

Those were wonderful movies. Truth always won. It's not like many of the movies of today, where evil is glorified and villains are made into heroes.

Those movies also taught us about the heroism of many of the people who built our country. I always admired their perseverance, energy, and the positive attitude it took to live like a pioneer.

Harvey had a cowboy hat, a gun belt, and cap guns. At the time, I collected story book dolls. Once, my mother bought me a set of cowboy and cowgirl dolls. Their eyes moved, and they were dressed in complete cowboy outfits, including hats. These meant so much to me when I was growing up. I still have these.

I fell in love with a few other things I saw in those movies. I was impressed with the wonderful dishes they had and always wanted a set. I discovered the pattern was called "Blue Willow" and has wonderful pictures of two turtle doves gazing at each other. The design comes from China, and there is a wonderful story about two lovers that goes with it. The tale says a girl eloped with her true love instead of marrying the wealthy man her father promised her to. Her father tracked them down, and as he was about to kill them, the gods transformed them into doves. Every cowboy movie I ever saw showed a set of these plates, and when I grew up and had the chance to collect a set for myself, I quickly picked them up.

I also admired how the cowboys always used real cloth napkins. Of course, in the old West, there wasn't much of a choice. But I was very impressed with the real cloth napkins I saw Dale and Roy use every week. I still use cloth napkins today, even though sometimes they are only bandanas.

No wonder my house has such a feel of the West. Watching, and admiring, the way our silver-screen heroes acted, had a profound impact on who I am today. When you enter the courtyard outside our front door, you are greeted by a beautiful clay statue of an Indian maiden. There are two wonderful dashes of turquoise on her, one on her head and one on the moccasin on her left foot that sticks out beneath her dress. She stands between a chiminea and a group of cacti nestled in a corner.

You can't help but notice all of the wonderful southwest flair throughout my house. These include a light fixture made from animal horns, a Native American festive dress hanging on the wall, and a beautiful water fountain nestled in the corner that looks like a large broken pot. Water cascades over the lip of the pot and trickles through pebbles in the base below.

My home has always been comfortable. When people come to see us, I want them to feel warm and invited, and that's one of the reasons I like the southwest style. It is hard to look at the soft colors and not feel comforted and invited.

It wasn't easy for me to leave Oklahoma because most of my family was here, and we had so many dear friends. It's never easy to walk away from your roots. But I should have known God was going to prepare me and, if I trusted Him, He would lead me to places I would never even have dreamed of on my own.

When we arrived in Albuquerque, we were excited to meet our new neighbors. The woman greeted me in tears, and had a warm smile spread across her face. She held her arms open and gave me a warm, loving embrace. We had never met, but her kind gestures helped create an immediate bond. I felt the presence of God that moment and knew I was standing in the place He meant for me to be. He had brought my wonderful new neighbor as an angel to help me with my transition.

We moved to a new neighborhood and were blessed with equally hospitable neighbors. When our daughter needed a tutor to help her with reading, one of them stepped in and helped. She was a professor at the University of New Mexico and was always willing to spend time helping us. She was also a gifted artist and painted a beautiful mural of Peter Rabbit in her children's nursery. They would bake cinnamon rolls and leave them for us as a special breakfast treat on Saturday mornings. They would put them on our porch and call to tell us our breakfast was ready. They went out of their way to make us feel welcome and cherished.

I came to understand why New Mexico is called The Land of Enchantment. It is one of those special places where you can see the hand of God everywhere you look. The pace of life is more relaxed, and you can't help but be grateful for all God has given you once you look out on the rolling high desert. Time seems to stand still there, and whenever I go, I feel like I am on lazy siesta time.

Every day, when the sun slowly creeps below the horizon, it casts a wonderful reddish hue on the mountains, and the trees look like they are burning. I appreciate why the mountains are named the Sangre de Cristo, or Blood of Christ.

Lisa, Beth, Gayle And Ludia.

Legacy

Roy and I tried to raise our children with the same work ethic we had. We wanted them to understand the value of friendship and to treat the people they worked with as family members. Our daughter, Lisa, started working as a baby sitter when she was just twelve. When she was in high school, she worked at a hospital. Roy eventually gave her permission to quit so she could have some time off.

It was also important that we be involved in our daughters' lives. I was the president of the PTA, a homeroom mom, and helped out with homework whenever I could. I owned the most used cookie sheets on the block, and I loved putting bandages on scraped knees and nursing broken hearts.

Roy and I were always a very good team, and we were naturally affectionate. Of course, we had problems like any couple, and I'm sure our children noticed when we were having a spat and weren't as affectionate as we usually were.

I don't think Roy and I were perfect, but the only thing I would do differently would be to show our daughters there are times when married people don't get along, and that's okay. Roy and I never talked about our problems in front of the girls. We would talk when we were alone and resolve things by ourselves. I now know this gave the appearance everything was perfect between Roy and me, and this gave our daughters the impression things would be perfect when they got married.

One of the reasons Roy and I got along so well was that we felt like we were there to protect each other. That's why we would discuss our problems in private. Our children should have seen how we talked things out with love and respect.

It came as a shock to my daughter Lisa when she got into her first argument with her husband two weeks into their marriage. It took time for her to learn to stand up for herself, and I'm sure Roy and I could have spared her this pain if we had been more open with our issues.

Lisa talks about how Roy put me up on a pedestal like a queen, and that he, "loved me to death." Roy was never a controlling man, he just wanted to spare me the pain and inconvenience of dealing with things. Our family never did without, he was a wonderful provider. He made life fun, and nothing made him happier than living with a complete family. He was, as Lisa called him, a "joyful spirit."

Roy and I taught our children family was important, and we worked hard to have healthy relationships with both of our daughters. I can only recall being angry at Lisa once as an adult. When I told her Ermon and I were getting married, she was not happy.

"You better live a long time," she told him. As I look back, I know it was not her who said those hurtful words, it was the pain of watching me lose two wonderful men, as well as her own pain from losing her father and another man she had come to love as a father.

Roy was very patient with the girls, and he taught Lisa how to drive. She loved this newfound freedom and would burn up a tank of gas on the weekends. He always encouraged her to learn new things.

Roy died three months before Lisa's wedding, and, like me, she knew something was wrong when the police came to our house.

She was very close to her father and the time after his death was a time of great emotional upheaval for her.

She felt like she had to be strong for the rest of us, and it took her some time before she could relax and find joy in life. Both of my daughters knew the time after Roy's death would be a period of great adjustment, and they both celebrated every time I learned to do something on my own.

I have taken a great joy in watching my daughters mature since their father's death. I have learned you can't force them to be who you want them to be. All you can do is to provide them with love, support, and guidance, and help them blossom into the people God created. I hope I have taught them to find the humor in every situation.

Like most young girls, Lisa wanted to get her ears pierced, and for some reason Roy was really opposed to this. She begged and begged, and I finally gave in, even though I knew my husband hadn't consented to it. When we came home, she tried really hard to hide her ears form her father. She tilted her head and tried to let her hair fall down and cover her lobes. It didn't take long for Roy to discover what was had happened, and he was not very happy. It took him awhile to accept what Lisa and I had done. Once he had calmed down, he extended a loving olive branch by buying Lisa a set of diamond studs.

I have always been very conscious about doing the things my parents and grandparents told me to do. I felt like if I were disobedient in any way, God would punish me. I am not sure where I got this idea. My family was always loving and supportive, and I grew up knowing God was kind and loving. But I always took words literally, especially when it came to the Bible, and I was especially sensitive to the commandment to, "honor your father and mother."

One thing Roy and I did well was to discipline our children. When I say discipline, I don't mean any kind of physical or mental abuse. But children will test limits, and when this happens it is important parents be willing to step up and let them know they have crossed the line. On the rare occasions I had to discipline my daughters I pinched the upper part of their arms. Not enough to hurt them or to leave any marks, but just enough to get their attention. I later learned they called it "the claw."

My daughter Beth loved attention. When we would go to the store, she would find her way to the service desk and tell the clerk she was lost just so she would hear her name called out over the loudspeaker. She also had to visit the restroom and look at it. Once, she was dared to put her tongue on a pole at the bus stop during the coldest part of winter. Her tongue froze to it and her cousin had to spit on it to get it to come off so she could get on the bus in time.

One Never Knew What A Vacation Would Produce.

Destinations

Roy and I got the girls a beagle, and they loved him. We couldn't find Beth one day, and went looking for her. We found her in the dog house, drinking out of his bowl. She told us she wanted to see what life was like for him.

Beth learned from watching her parents that she didn't want any drama in life. She was a "daddy's girl," and his death was hard for her.

One of the most valuable lessons he taught her was to, "learn something from everything you go through." This has been valuable advice as Beth has recently faced many medical issues. Although I would never wish health issues on anyone, especially my own daughter, I am proud of how she has handled the challenges that have come her way.

I am also proud both of my daughters are wonderful mothers.

Lisa is blessed with a son, Josh. Beth has a son and a daughter, Dalton and Katie. All of my grandchildren have blossomed because their families love and care for them so much.

One of Beth's favorite memories is from a trip we took to Carlsbad Caverns. As we made our way down the winding path inside the cave, something got stuck in Lisa's shoe, and she kicked it off. It almost flew beyond the railing to the bottom of the cave.

I can understand why Beth remembers this. I also remember my first trip to Carlsbad. I must have been eight or nine years old. We walked down the mouth of the cave as far as they would let us and had our group stand in a circle. They turned out the lights and, in the pitch black that wouldn't let you see your hand in front of your face, we all sang "Rock of Ages." It was an awesome experience to hear the words echo off the walls and added to the majesty of the moment.

It's funny what little details stick in your mind. Roy and I took the girls on a trip to Galveston Beach in south Texas. We stopped at a little restaurant called "Guido's" and ate the best blueberry pie. On the way back, we stopped at "Gilley's" in Dallas, the club where they filmed the movie "Urban Cowboy." That was a real thrill for the girls.

Beth and her father loved spending time together. One of their favorite things was to go the local Sears store. They would buy candy and spend the afternoon together. Roy loved going there to shop for tools, and I'm sure Beth learned a lot about wrenches and saws during those lazy afternoons.

We lived in Colorado for a brief time near my brother Harvey. Our kids would ride four-wheelers together. They spent hours on those machines, and didn't quit until they ran out of gas.

In the evening, they would walk from house to house and ask what was for dinner. Once they knew their options, they would stop at the place that had the best menu.

Beth has always had a flair for the dramatic. She even calls herself my "diva daughter." When we lived in Albuquerque, we once threw her a birthday party at an ice cream parlor, and she got so embarrassed she hid under the table. When she was in the first grade, I got a call from her teacher. Beth was upset and crying because she wanted her teacher to call her "Penelope" when she called roll. Somehow she had it set in her mind her name was Penelpoe and didn't want to be called by anything else.

Beth once told me she hopes to be one-half or even one-quarter of the woman I am. What mother could expect her daughter to say such sweet things? I want both of my daughters to understand how special they are and what amazing women they have become.

Beth used to go fishing with Roy. Sometimes they would bring a friend and make a weekend as they cast their lines and waited for the fish to bite.

When we lived in Colorado, God taught me one of the greatest lessons I have ever learned. I went out on the patio behind our house and watched a big caterpillar as it inched along. A few days later, I came out and noticed it had encased itself in its pupa. It struggled to free itself, and I desperately wanted to help it, but I knew I wasn't supposed to. That's how it gets its strength, by fighting through the hard shell. If I reached down and freed it, I might help it for a moment, but in the long run I would do more damage than good. It eventually emerged as a bright red butterfly and was as big as a platter. I close my eyes and I can still see it flap its wings and take flight.

I knew God was trying to teach me a lesson, and I thought of how parents can hinder the growth of their children by being overprotective. Love means giving your children the wings they need to fly out of the nest when God calls them to.

We had a good life, and still do, in spite of the heartache and tragedy. We learned to live from it. How you choose to respond makes all the difference in the world. I choose to be happy.

Sometimes it feels like Roy's passing was just yesterday, but sometimes it is something misty and very far away. I love my children and the life I have been given. My heart is so full, I can't be thankful enough for it.

Roy's Headstone.

Dreams

After Roy and I had been married for over twenty years, I felt the urge to become a bit more independent. This was nothing rebellious or disrespectful, but I got in my head I should have my own credit card. Roy wasn't excited about this, but we talked it over and I finally managed to fill out and mail an application. Sure enough, a few weeks later, the card came in the mail with my name on it. I was so proud.

It was also put on my heart to start my own business. With Roy's help, I opened a small gift and antique shop in 1982. I was thrilled to have my own place where I could collect and sell so many of the wonderful things that caught my eye that would never fit in my home.

Roy was always very supportive of me. I can't think of one time when he discouraged me or wasn't willing to help me reach my goals. When the opportunity arose for me to take part in An Affair of the Heart in 1985, he was glad for me. Many men would feel threatened by an ambitious wife who wanted to be successful, but I can honestly say Roy was never intimidated. He loved watching me start and build the shop, and got caught up in the excitement of the show as much as I did.

After the show had been running for a year, in the beginning of 1986, I had a turning point in my faith. I had been raised in the church and always loved the Lord and wanted to live the life He had created for me. I wanted to make sure my life was a testament to Him, and I made it a priority to draw close to Him every day.

At the start of the new year, like many people, I made a resolution to become closer to God. I started praying daily that God help me become all I could be for Him. I asked Him to remove anything in my life that stood between Him and me. I was willing to be and do everything just for Him.

About the same time, I started having vivid dreams about losing my purse. In each of these dreams, I would franticly dig throughout the house trying to find it, but never could. I would wake up from these dreams, reach over and touch my husband, to make sure he was alive. This went on for three weeks, and the entire time I was anxious and knew something wasn't right. I couldn't put my finger on it, but my life felt out of balance and unpredictable. It was a very unsettling feeling.

About the same time, one of my daughters started dreaming about her father dying. As I look back, I see God was preparing me for the loss of my financial security, my husband. God was telling me what was going to happen so I would have the strength to step through the door and enter the next phase of my life. It seems so clear now, but at the time I was so uncertain and afraid.

There was nothing unusual about the morning of March 12, 1986. Roy and I woke up, ate our breakfast, and he headed to work. I expected him back around 1:30 that afternoon, and even baked his favorite cake, a "lazy daisy." This was a recipe from Roy's family, one his mother and aunts always made. It is a white cake with a coconut frosting. After you spread the frosting on top, you place under the broiler for a moment and the coconut get slightly brown and just a little crunchy. He loved that cake and enjoyed having it as a special treat.

One-thirty came and went, and Roy had still not come home. I became concerned. He was very punctual, and if he was running behind schedule, he would have called me and let me know. I knew something was wrong when he didn't make it home on time. I tried to keep my mind occupied by doing chores around the quiet house.

The doorbell rang, and I braced myself. I walked to the front door and looked outside. A red-headed female police officer was standing at my doorway, and I froze. At that moment, I knew Roy was gone. She didn't have to say a word. The dreams my daughter and I had been having for the last few weeks flashed before me, and I knew that somehow, this was what God had been preparing me for. I didn't understand why it was happening. I only knew it was how God intended my life to be.

I strained to reach for the handle and slowly pushed the door open. The officer, Janet Hogue, stepped into our home.

She struggled to speak to me. It took her three times before she could ask, "Mrs. Bowling?"

"It's Roy, isn't it?" I asked. I knew he was gone even before Officer Hogue said another word.

"Yes. There's been an accident. He has died."

With those simple words, my entire life (and the lives of

my two beautiful daughters), came crashing down. I felt everything drain from me. All of my hopes and dreams took flight, and I stood there with Officer Hogue feeling cold and numb. After twenty-eight and one-half years of marriage, I was a widow, alone and afraid.

I could see how much pain she was in. Her face and eyes told me she was grieving with me. I later found out this was the very first time she had to deliver such terrible news to anyone.

In spite of just hearing my that husband had died, I knew Janet was hurting, too. I could see how sad and scared she was. I did my best to comfort her and ignored my own suffering. We stood there, two women in pain, each trying to help the other fight through the terrible moment.

Janet and I have a forever bond after that. She even came to work for us at the show as a security officer for a few years, and each time we see each other we are reminded of how God puts special people together, if only for a short time and under heartbreaking circumstances.

Another special person who came into my life during this period was Gary James. I didn't know him, but Gary worked at the show as a security guard for several years. He eventually pulled me aside.

"There is something I need to tell you," he said. He went on to explain he was the officer who investigated Roy's death. He had the responsibility of examining the scene, looking at the body, and determining the cause of death. He told me about this with such love and care that I will never forget him or the kindness he showed me and my family. Gary is a special man, and he is another example of a person God put in my life at a certain time and for a certain reason. I have always valued his friendship and caring.

I started the morning of Roy's death following the plan I had always dreamed of. I had two beautiful children, one of whom was getting married in the summer. The other was in her junior year of high school. I had a wonderful home and owned a business I loved and knew would grow. My life looked like the picture painted in my head, and we had so many special times waiting for us.

I never got to say goodbye to Roy. His death was sudden and unexpected, and when he left that morning I had no idea it would be the last time I see would him. I wish I could hug him one more time and thank him for the time he gave me and the example he set for our daughters.

By the time my head hit the pillow that night, I was a widow and had no idea how I was going to move forward. Everything in my life had been turned upside down. All of the security and peace I had known were wrestled from me, and there was nothing I could do to change it. All of the reference points from the road map I was following had suddenly vanished, and I didn't know where I was going or how I was going to get there. I didn't see a life beyond that moment, and I couldn't grasp how I was going to move forward. I thought my life was over.

I now understand this was not the end. It was a beginning.

Learning, Growing And Taking Flight.

Taking Flight

Life will bring you moments when you think your road, the path you have always traveled, has come to an end. You may sit with your head in your hands as tears roll down your cheeks not knowing how to take your next step. You don't know which way to go, or if there is even anywhere else you can go. You may think you will never move beyond that moment.

I have learned these moments are not dead-ends, but they are on-ramps to different roads that will take you to places you never dreamed. Places that are more beautiful than you could have imagined and with treasures beyond the pictures in your head or the desires of your heart.

But sometimes you won't see this until you have put a few

miles in your rear-view mirror. And it can be scary sitting at a stop sign in the middle of the night when you think the place you were going is no longer an option.

If I was going to survive after Roy died, I knew I had to learn many things in a short period of time. It was a period of accelerated growth for me. I don't know if I have ever learned as much in such a concentrated time.

Roy had taken care of all of us, me and the girls, and there were so many things he had done that we took for granted. I had never filled my own car with gas and didn't know how to do this. I had taken out the trash no more than one or two times in my entire life. These had always been Roy's job, and I had to learn how to do them on my own. And then there were the more important things, like paying the bills.

I also was surprised how his death had changed many of the relationships in my life. Many of my friends had only known me as part of a couple. They had never known me outside of my marriage to Roy. When that ended, it was difficult for us to relate to one another. Even people in my church struggled with this. When I lost Roy, I also lost most of the closeness and intimacy we had enjoyed with these couples. That's natural and I mean no disrespect when I say these things.

I later found out my friends and family were very worried about me. They had no idea how I would react to being a widow and didn't know if I would be able to make it on my own.

I prayed constantly during this period, and wanted God to show me why Roy had to be taken from me. God eventually helped me accept the change that had been forced upon me. God also let me know He would provide the strength I needed and there was another life waiting for me.

If I sat around feeling sorry for myself, I would never step through the door and claim my new life. Most people don't want change. They want things to be the same forever and ever, and that's how I felt after Roy's death. I wanted things to go back the way they were, they way I had always dreamed they should be.

But I soon realized change can be your friend. Once I accepted that, I began to heal. Had I not accepted and welcomed the fact my life had changed forever, I would have missed an amazing journey.

My healing took place an inch at a time. One small step I took was to start sitting in a different seat in church. Like many people, Roy and I always sat in the same area with the same people when we worshiped. There's nothing wrong with this, it's just how people act. We like familiar places and faces. So changing seats forced me to reconsider everything about my spiritual life, including all the relationships Roy and I had built over the years.

One of my greatest challenges was to go to a restaurant and eat all alone. This may sound silly, but when you are used to eating every meal with your husband and then become a widow, eating alone is one of the most difficult transitions to make. Many people have told me they couldn't do it. Some had tried, but seeing an empty chair across the table was too painful. Others felt self-conscious about going into a dining room by themselves. It was difficult to tell the waiter they were there alone, and it was even worse feeling the stares of people who were eating and laughing with their families.

But I knew if I didn't have the courage to go to a restaurant and eat alone, my life would be very limited, and I wasn't going to let that happen to me. So I eventually got the courage to eat a meal all alone.

God doesn't expect us to sit and wait for Him to bring things to us. He gave us tools, talents, and skills to make things happen. I knew it was up to me to embrace the change and to do the best with what I had.

Gayle's Car Purchase.

Wheels

I eventually needed a new car. I had never bought one. Roy had always taken care of that. A car would be the first major purchase I made on my own. I took Daddy to the dealership with me for moral support, but I chose the car I wanted and did all the negotiating. Driving off the lot with my new car was such a feeling of accomplishment. I felt like I had done the greatest thing in the world. I wanted to thank the bank for loaning me the money. I felt so blessed, not only to be able to pay for it with money I had made on my own, but also knowing God had given me the strength and courage to make it happen. This gave me such a boost of self-confidence, and I knew I was going to survive.

Another thing I had to learn was that I could not be both a mother and a father to my daughters. I am a very nurturing person, especially with my own family. When someone close to me is hurting, I want to spread my wings around them and cover them from the wind and rain. But I couldn't fill the gap created when their father was gone, no matter how hard I tried. I had to learn to let this go so I could focus on being a complete mother to the girls and giving them 100 percent of their mother's love. That's all I had to offer.

I will never forget the night before Roy's funeral. My mother came to comfort me, and we talked until the wee hours of the morning. I prayed that night, hoping God would show me why a loving, faithful husband had been taken from his wife and children and what purpose this tragedy had. I woke up seeing a bright light, and feeling nothing but love and peace.

My mom sat up in her bed and touched my face. "What has happened to you?" she said. "You're all . . . shiny."

God touched me that night. He came to me and gave me comfort and strength. I felt the warmth and sustenance of His grace, and my mother could see this just by looking at my beaming face.

If you have a true servant's heart, and are willing to give

yourself to others, even if it means "washing their feet," you can use even the darkest of times to help them grow. I tried to remember that when Roy passed away.

The week of the funeral, I was blessed to have one of my dear friends, Linda Jeary, come to my house during my time of need. We talked and laughed and cried, and as time went by it became clear to me she did not know the Lord. I don't take any credit for this, but I was able to use the time we had together to help Linda become a Christian. Now she was not only one of my best friends, she was also my sister in Christ.

I had the privilege of working with her and mentoring her over the course of the next few years.

One of the best things I did for myself after Roy passed away was to enroll in a women's career development program at a local community college. This was designed for women in transition. They had classes for the newly widowed, like me, as well as women who were divorced or were looking to make career changes.

I was in the very first class they offered. It really forced me to stretch myself and to think about what could be, instead of thinking about what might have been. I took these lessons and applied them in my business, and after it flourished I was fortunate to come back to the program and be a mentor.

Within the weeks that followed Roy's passing, working through the emotional pain was difficult. On many days, I felt physically ill.

I held on tightly to the scripture as I wept during the night, "that joy would come in the morning." How I wanted the morning to come.

As I struggled to embrace the change in my life, I began to think what if I tried to look more on the positive rather than the negative side of the situation. I did not want this point to become a "comfort zone" that I could not move out of.

As uncomfortable as it was to let go of how I had always done things, I slowly began to move forward. I began by changing where I sat in church on Sunday. There was a feeling as I established my new place to sit that half of me was gone. I became much more aware of loneliness as I made changes. My perspective on who I was began to change. My identity as part of a couple was completely stripped away.

One of the most difficult choices I had to make was to move to a smaller house. The girls and I no longer needed as much space as we did when Roy was living, and there were also financial pressures. I couldn't afford the house we had without Roy's income.

It was so difficult for us to pack all of our memories and put them in moving boxes. When we closed the front door of the house for the final time, I was heading to a place I had never been before. I was moving into my own place, the only one I had ever picked out and paid for by myself. It was truly going to be my nest, and the thought was daunting.

Just as God can take the clay and mold it, I felt like the broken vessel ready to be used for His purpose. I prayed every day for wisdom and that I would live my life for His will, not my own. I was rapidly learning the pain would move on towards the "joy in the morning" when I allowed His wisdom to take over my being completely. Learning to treat change as a friend and not as an enemy can bring to us unexpected opportunities and happiness.

I sometimes wonder what would have happened if Roy had not passed away. How different would my life be? He was always very supportive of me, and I know if he had seen how the show has grown he would be filled with pride. But I wonder if I would have been willing to take the chances and pushed myself to the same level of success had his death not forced me to.

Wyane And Gayle.

Wayne

After Roy passed away, I knew I would have to find work. I had the show, and it was beginning to grow, but it was not a full-time job. I love to work. It keeps me focused and energized. I had to find something that would keep me busy. I'm not the kind of person who wants to sit at home with nothing to do. In fact, one of the things I have recently done is to create a "five-year plan" so I have goals and direction for the next part of my life. This is actually part of a larger "twenty-five year plan." Even though I am entering the late fall of my life, I have no intention of being idle.

After Roy died, I did everything I could to stay busy. I worked for a friend who was a florist, I worked for my insurance agent, and I eventually found a job leasing apartments.

I applied at an upscale women's clothing store. After the manager reviewed my application, I was shocked to hear what she said.

"I'm sorry. You can't work here. You're over-qualified."

I never could figure that out. Isn't the purpose of hiring people to bring in the most qualified and experienced people you can? But I didn't let that get me down. I had enough faith in God and my own abilities and knew I would survive.

When I started working at the apartment complex, I soon met Wayne Chambers, who was in charge of the fitness room. He was also a very talented artist, and made Christmas decorations the complex displayed throughout the holidays.

At first, I ran from Wayne. I didn't want to take the chance on loving again. There is a perception in our society if you find true love, you will ride off into the sunset and everything will be perfect. I used to believe this. I was taught this as a child.

Sometimes, we look at successful people and think, "They have it all." That's not what we really mean. I think we really mean they only have half of everything. We are led to believe enough money or fame can keep us from the natural pain in life, like death, illness, and disappointment. After Roy's death, I knew that wasn't the case and I wanted to shield myself in every way I could.

When Wayne and I met, neither one of us was ready to commit to anything serious. A relationship was the last thing on either of our minds. I was a widow, and he had gone through a divorce. We began by being friends, and as we felt comfortable and trusting of each other, these feelings developed into romantic ones.

When Wayne came into my life and I was finally willing to open my heart again, I was amazed at what God gave us. God accelerated what time we had. We only knew each other for seven years, but we managed to fill them with a lifetime of love, joy, and memories.

Wayne had battled his own set of demons. Long before we met, he tried to commit suicide. One night he swallowed a bunch of pills and hoped his days on this earth were over. But God wasn't finished with him. When Wayne survived to the next day, he knew God had plans for him and he worked each and every day after that to find and fulfill his purpose.

When Wayne and I decided to marry, I bought him a nice pair of ostrich cowboy boots. If you have never seen a pair of those, they are wonderfully luxurious. They are a warm, supple brown, and the leather has wonderful bumps where the quills have been removed.

We eloped to Vegas, which was a little out of character for me. Wayne was much more spontaneous than I was, and those who knew us would appreciate that. Most of my friends would have guessed I would have stayed in Oklahoma City and had a nice ceremony at my church. To be honest, our families were disappointed. They wanted to share in this special moment and were saddened we didn't give them the chance.

When we returned to Oklahoma City, we held a reception and celebration for our families and friends. My friend Connie Harris helped me produce this, and all of our gracious friends and family forgave us for eloping.

As I mentioned, Wayne had overcome his own share of struggles. Long before I knew him, he recognized he had a drinking problem and got the help he needed. He had been a recovering alcoholic for twenty-two years at the time of his death. Once he conquered his drinking problem, he wanted to help others. He knew how difficult it was to overcome addiction and felt his experiences could benefit others. Wayne would help anyone who needed it and wanted to be an example to others of what they could become.

He eventually became the first drug, alcohol, and substance abuse counselor at one of our local hospitals. He devoted his time there to helping doctors and lawyers who had succumbed to temptation.

He was always very strong with his recovery and knew he had to take it day by day to stay sober. It never bothered him to be around others who were drinking because he felt comfortable with the changes he made to his life. In fact, one of our friends sent a bottle of champagne to us during our honeymoon. I didn't drink any of it. In fact, I didn't drink the entire time we were together. Before Wayne came into my life, I enjoyed an occasional glass of wine, but I gave that up when we started dating. It would have bothered me to kiss him with alcohol on my breath. I didn't want to be a stumbling block for him, and I didn't want to do something he would never be able to enjoy. I think it would have been cruel to have taken a sip of alcohol in front of him.

If I had to choose one word to describe our time together, it would be "fun." We tried to make the most of every moment, and I cherished the days we spent together. There were two things Wayne always wanted to do. One was to buy a red Corvette. Every time we would see one he would smile and talk about how we could get him one.

His other dream was to take me to Vietnam, which he called "the Paris of the Orient." Wayne had been stationed there when he was in the military, and he came to love this country. His face would light up as he told me about the people, the smells, and the food. He loved it so much he became fluent in Vietnamese. I wish he could have lived long enough to make this dream come true.

Another Birdhouse Wayne Made.

Birdhouses

Wayne was also an extremely talented man. One of the things he did was to design and build birdhouses that looked like the wonderful adobe houses you see in the southwest, like New Mexico and Arizona. Wayne paid painstaking attention to every detail. He made sure his houses had vigas, the round logs used as ceiling beams that stick out on the sides, and canales, the little spouts that let the water escape during the rare New Mexico rainstorms, just like they do on the real houses. He made small ladders, and even created little ristras, the bunches of chili peppers that hang and dry outside of so many houses and businesses. We got to know people at a weaving shop in Chimayo, a tiny community in northern New

Mexico famous for its wool and rugs, and asked them for scraps so Wayne could make small rugs. The exteriors of the birdhouses were coved in real stucco we bought and took back to Oklahoma.

On some of trips we would stop for hot chocolate in La Fonda, a wonderful hotel on the old plaza in Santa Fe. There is a cozy little restaurant just off of the street facing the plaza, and we loved nestling in there whenever we got the chance. We would sometimes walk to the hotel during a snowfall and as the snowflakes flitted about in the breeze we would catch them on our tongues. It was a wonderful feeling to walk out of the cold and into the warmth coming from the fireplace.

It was really like two separate restaurants. In the morning, you could watch people as they prepared for the day. The room filled with happy chatter and the smell of fresh bread enticed us. In the evening, it was just warm and inviting.

Wayne never met a stranger and loved talking to the people we met there. He always found out where they were from and what they did for a living. Some of them were locals coming to visit one of their favorite haunts. Others were skiers in town to enjoy the fresh powder in the mountains, and we met other people who had come from all around the world to enjoy the mystique of the Southwest. Regardless of who we were with, we always relished the peace, and we loved sitting and talking over our hot chocolate. We sometimes shared these trips with our friends, Larry and Nancy Nelson, who loved Santa Fe as much as we did. When Larry gave the eulogy at Wayne's funeral, I thought of the many precious nights we had spent talking and laughing at La Fonda.

Wayne soon came to love New Mexico as much as I did. We started displaying luminaries at Christmas time. These are little bags that are illuminated with candles. They are a southwest tradition and during the holidays you can see them line streets and driveways. We had so much fun doing this each year.

We visited the Grand Canyon together. We rode the train from Williams, Arizona to the South Rim. We laughed all the way there, and the entire ride made us feel like we were in the old West. The train company even staged a fake train robbery, and the "outlaws" boarded the train and tried to take our loot. They then led us all in songs.

As you may have noticed, I love dramatic, sweeping places. The entire Southwest is like that to me. The Grand Canyon gave

Wayne and me a feeling I can't describe. When you stand on the edge and watch the colors come to life as the sun moves across the sky, it is hard not to feel God speaking to you. I will never forget the layers of pink and green rocks that peek out above the rushing waters of the Colorado River.

On our train ride out of Williams, Wayne and I watched the landscape crawl by as the train chugged over the tracks. I felt like I could reach out and touch God. It was a very spiritual experience, and I know everyone on the trip felt the same way. A quiet, calm hush came over us, and it was easy to feel the reverence and awe we experienced.

Wayne's birdhouses were really works of art and should have been kept inside, but Wayne did occasionally put one outside. We used one as a mailbox, and people would occasionally ask us if they could buy one.

Wayne became intensely focused on making these little birdhouses realistic, and he wouldn't let anything get in his way. After he had been making them for a while, he wanted to find a way to make the weathering look real. He wanted people to think the houses had been baking beneath the clear, blue New Mexico sky for years. Somehow, he discovered the perfect solution. After he stained them, he put the parts in one of my best white pillowcases (of course), threw it into a clothes dryer, and let it bounce around for awhile. He managed to turn my clothes dryer into a giant commercial tumbler.

He was right, when the parts came out, they looked just like he wanted. What he didn't think about was how they beat up the inside of the dryer or how the stain seeped through the bag and stuck to the drum of the dryer. The dryer was ruined. I was not happy, to put it mildly, and told him so.

"Don't worry about it. I'll buy you a new dryer," he said as he shrugged his shoulders. He did just that, but he kept the old one and incorporated it into his birdhouse empire.

We always bought the stucco for the birdhouses in Santa Fe and brought it back to Oklahoma with us. During one of these trips, we got caught in a snowstorm. The flakes were coming down so heavily we had to pull over for the night and stay in a hotel. We hauled the stucco into our hotel room so it would not freeze during the night.

When the storm was at its worst, we could barely see the road in front of us and had to follow a semi-truck to make our way. I was able to make out something on the back of the truck and smiled.

"What are we following?" I asked.

"A truck," Wayne said.

"No, look at the back of the truck." I pointed to a big red cross painted on one of its back doors. "Just keep following the cross."

Wayne.

Goodwill

Those little birdhouses sold really well, and we even took out an ad in a Japanese magazine. Wayne was so excited about the way his birdhouses were received, and it warmed my heart to see him and his business blossom. We had the entire business in our garage, and one side was devoted to manufacturing (Wayne's domain) and the other to marketing (my territory). We even had a little chute that hung from the ceiling in our garage and dispensed Styrofoam packing peanuts to protect the birdhouses when they were shipped. As sales took off, we eventually had to move the operation to a warehouse.

We did such a good job, Wayne eventually was able to have

the bird houses sold in a gift shop in Taos. I remember how warm and inviting the shop was when we visited. That was a real blessing. There are highly trained and respected artists from all over the world who never have the chance to get their work sold and displayed in New Mexico. The fact that Wayne was able to do this with no formal training is a testament to how gifted he was.

We were also able to get the birdhouses sold in a shop in Arizona, as well as in a kiosk in a mall in Santa Fe. They even appeared in an edition of "Cowboys and Indians," a respected magazine that caters to people who love the west and all things western.

Our major coup, though, was getting Wayne and his birdhouses invited to appear on HGTV as part of a special they did on "Made in Oklahoma" products. The TV station sent a crew to film here, and Wayne's products were featured on television. While the show aired, we sold over 500 birdhouses in twenty-eight minutes.

This was a fun, but wild time. Every so often my parents would come around to check on our production line. Wayne loved showing them all the things we were able to do.

As I explained, Wayne was passionate about helping other people who were struggling with addiction and recovery. Many of his employees were referred by the transitional house at the local Goodwill. Wayne was so appreciative of them and wanted to show them how much he cared one Christmas. He bought boxes and boxes of fruit and nuts, just like we used to have for Christmas when we were children. Wayne, my parents, and I made gift bags and took them to all the men who worked in the warehouse. It warmed Wayne's heart to be able to do that, and he was truly grateful for their help.

Wayne was a great teacher to these men, and also to me. I learned so much form him during this time. I saw how easily some people can slide into addiction and how it can break spirits and ruin lives. But I also learned that, with God's help, we can overcome anything. There is no mistake so large it cannot be overcome with faith, prayer, and determination. It was special to see this side of Wayne. I hope those who knew him before he got sober realize how much he had changed and how he helped others turn their lives around.

I never really thought about it, but Wayne must have had an issue with laundry. Not only did he ruin our perfectly good washer, but he was the world's worst at using bleach. Whenever he did a load of white clothes, he always thought it needed just a little more bleach. One time, he didn't check the washer to see if there were any clothes in it before he loaded his whites. By the end of the wash cycle, my favorite pair of brown slacks had been ruined.

"Oh, that color is not so bad," he said when I paraded the faded pants before him.

"Would you wear these?" I asked. Needless to say, Wayne replaced the pants.

During our marriage, I was proud to witness Wayne's baptism. Not only was he my husband, he was my brother in Christ. We had a copy of the Bible on our computer, and he spent hours scouring it and tilling the soil of his soul with God's word. He absorbed every word like a sponge.

I used to put little notes in Wayne's lunches. I still have stacks of messages we passed back and forth.

He also became a passionate golfer after being introduced to the gentleman's game by his dear friend, Al Lovelace. Even thought he didn't start playing until he was older, Wayne eventually shot three holes-in-one. He was the only grandfather my grandchildren had ever known, and he loved taking them golfing with him. Wayne loved the fact that the boys referred to us as, "Mimi and Papa Wayne." He loved how he was accepted as part of our family.

Wayne wasn't vain, but he did care about his appearance. It was important to him that he looked good whenever he went out. And he always wore cologne. Some of my friends joked that when we got married, I had to get a bigger mirror for the house.

As Wayne got older, he underwent two open-heart surgeries. I helped him recover from the second one, and we were able to have some honest, open, and deep conversations. There is something liberating about hospitals. People who are really ill or injured lose any pretention or reservations they might normally have and can be more open and honest with their friends and families. As he sat in his hospital bed, Wayne told me the seven years we spent together were the happiest and most satisfying of his life. I am so grateful God put us together so I could help Wayne achieve his goals. God put me in his life to bring out the best in Wayne.

We had talked about his funeral long before we needed to. My brother Harvey had purchased a dozen funeral plots in Paul's Valley, a wonderful community about halfway between Oklahoma City and Dallas, Texas. After we were married, I asked Wayne if he wanted to be buried there. I knew that's where I will find my final resting place and I wanted Wayne to know he had that option.

"I'll think about it," he told me.

I had almost forgotten about it until one day he said, "I've thought about it. I want to be buried in your family plot." I wasn't sure what he meant and he had to remind me of our conversation.

"The way I have it figured," he said with a smile, "is if I'm on one side of you and Roy is on the other, I think we can keep you in line."

What a great response. People shouldn't be afraid of death. It's not an ending, it's a beginning. I've come to believe cemeteries are God's gardens. Caskets are not boxes to be thrown into the ground and covered with dirt. They are hope chests, and they contain reminders of the most wonderful things we have collected during our time on Earth. They remind us of the hope we have in God for eternal life.

Unfortunately, in December of 1999, Wayne suffered a debilitating stroke. His recovery didn't go as well as we had hoped, and he got sicker and sicker. He eventually got so sick he couldn't speak, and his systems began shutting down. I was practically living at the hospital, staying as close as I could to him.

I eventually had to accept that Wayne was going to be sent to a long-term care facility. My spontaneous, loving, vibrant husband would no longer be able to care for himself or enjoy many of the things we had done together. I didn't want to make that decision. I would have hated seeing him like that, and I knew he would have hated being in that condition.

God intervened and spared us both. Wayne's doctor was truly an angel, and he recognized Wayne would not have wanted to be confined to a bed with no chance of enjoying a sunset or a conversation with one of his friends again.

The doctor sat down with me and told me Wayne was not going to recover and a very difficult choice had to be made. "But I want you to understand, I am making this decision, not you." His compassion, understanding, and sensitivity spared me and Wayne a great deal of sorrow and regret.

On Wayne's last day, his brother, sister, ex-wife, and children came to the hospital. I didn't know it then, but now I understand this was all part of God's plan. I was completely rundown, and I must have looked like I had been rode hard and put up wet. Wayne's family told me to go home, rest, and take a shower. My heart was really heavy about this. I didn't want to leave Wayne's side at the time he needed me the most, and they really had to convince me it was okay to leave.

As soon as I sat on my couch at home, Wayne's brother called with the news he had passed away.

After the doctor gave us the freedom to let Wayne go, and while I was at our house, my second husband went home to be with the Lord.

The Mailbox Wayne Made For Our Home.

Grace

I went back to the hospital as quickly as I could. I stepped into the elevator and frantically pushed the button to get back to my husband. As the elevator rose and the door opened on the next floor, I was face to face with Wayne's ex-wife and children. They were very distraught over Wayne's death. I then understood why God wanted me to allow them to have the time alone with Wayne during his final moments. It pains me because I felt like I had left my husband at his most desperate hour. But God had other plans, and that meant I had to let go of what I wanted so He could give others what they needed. That's the way life is. Sometimes you have to take less than what you want so that those around you can have their needs met. It's not always easy, but that's how it has to be.

I was devastated. I had trusted the Lord and felt like I was being obedient to His commands. But here I was, planning another funeral for a man I loved. Why would God bring these men to me and let me fall so deeply in love with them, only to let both of them go when there was so much time left?

I have come to understand every person in my life has served a different and valuable purpose, and this is God's plan. When we face a loss, we sometimes can't see through the cloud of pain and sorrow, and it can be impossible to find God's plan in anything. When we let time pass and put some distance between ourselves and tragedy, God's majesty unfolds before us. Knowing this and understanding it as an adult shows us life is not perfect and complete.

All of our relationships wax and wane, and this is true even of our relationship with God. Some days, we feel like we can crawl up on God's lap, and we feel Him laugh as He squeezes and kisses us. Other days, we struggle to hear His voice as we stumble in the darkness hoping to find a way out of the wilderness, not knowing He is walking beside us the entire time.

God is always there for us. When we are joyful, He celebrates with us. When we are brokenhearted, He puts us back together. I have lost count of how many times my Heavenly Father has loved me and repaired me. Sometimes, I say the time after Wayne's death felt as if I were walking through the desert. I had to force myself to put one foot in front of the other, slogging through an arid, lifeless land with no end in sight.

At the funeral, we sprayed Wayne's casket with his cologne. That way, everyone could close their eyes, and the smell would remind them of all the wonderful memories they had with him. Wayne's favorite golfing buddies, our grandchildren, asked to keep the cologne to remember him by.

After the dust settled, we put Wayne's earthly body into the ground. He was laid to rest in our family plot in Paul's Valley, right next to Roy. Some men might be offended to be buried next to their wife's first husband. But Wayne and Roy would have liked it. I'm sure they felt like I was introducing them to each other.

Grieving over the loss of two men has taught me many things, and I learned a great deal about myself. When bad news comes along, I can be like a cat. I leap into action when danger approaches. Something just clicks and I hit the floor running.

I don't look for bad things to happen, and I am a very optimistic person. But I have also learned to be prepared for the difficulties that will come into my life. All of us, regardless of where we live or how we act, are going to face challenging times when things do not go our way. Don't run from these. Embrace them as a time to take action, make changes, and draw closer to God. Whatever you do, don't avoid dealing with bad times. Your life is too short for you to keep running from the painful things you will face. If you try to avoid obstacles, you deny yourself the chance to grow and become a better person.

I always valued the time I spent with Wayne's family. I loved him completely, and that included his first wife and children. After Wayne and I were married, I sat down with Wayne's children. I knew it was difficult for them to see their father with another woman. Divorce is difficult for any family, and children seem to bear the brunt when their parents decide to end a marriage.

I told them I would do anything, including giving up their father, if it would make their family whole again. I meant every word of it. I know God wants whole, complete families, and if it were God's will for Wayne to reconcile with the mother of his children, I would have accepted it and been thankful for the time we had together. That was a heart-wrenching thing for me to say, but I meant every word of it.

After Wayne died, I wasn't able to keep the close relationship with his children we enjoyed when he was with us, and that still hurts me. I hope, if they read these words, God will move all of our hearts to reconcile, and we can once again share the love and joy Wayne would want us to.

Before Wayne passed away, while he was in the hospital, his first wife gave me one of the most beautiful gifts I have ever received. She thanked me for the time I gave Wayne and for being so kind to her children. She also told me the time Wayne and I had spent together was special. She knew how happy he was and how much we had both blossomed when we were together. She also said she knew this was something she could not have given him.

As I look back, I am amazed at her ability to say this. She was an incredibly confident, gracious, beautiful, and loving person. Many people would not have had the strength to give any compliment to the person that married their former spouse. For her to look me in the eye and say such loving things speaks well to her strength and to her love for Wayne and their children.

One day I will join Roy and Wayne in the cemetery in Paul's Valley. But hopefully that won't happen for some time. I have a twenty-five year plan to complete!

When we were at the cemetery, after the service was over, I spoke with our funeral director. Humor has always been important to me. It is a gift God has given us and it brings us joy and helps heal us when we feel defeated. Some people may think it is wrong or disrespectful to use humor at a funeral, but I think it is life affirming.

"I've done my part," I told the director. "Don't expect me to fill this whole cemetery up."

I still have one of Wayne's birdhouse lamps sitting in my living room. Each time I see it perched there, I can't help but think about how blessed we were to have our time together and how fortunate I was to walk the same road with him, if only for a short while.

Ermon.

Ermon

After Wayne passed away, I was blessed to have a third wonderful man come into my life. How we met is another example of how God takes tragedy and turns it into beauty.

About a year after Wayne died, I served as a Vice-President on our neighborhood association. Friends and family told me I needed to be busy, and I took the position so they would see I was adjusting after Wayne's death.

One of our meetings was held at the house of the president, Ermon Dyer. During a break in the meeting, I went into his kitchen to get a drink. I opened up his kitchen cabinets to find a glass. As I looked at the plates nestled on the shelf, my face turned white and I quickly shut the door.

Some people may think this sounds crazy, but I have a set of dishes that are adorned with a beautiful southwest pattern. A jagged green band is drawn around the outside edge of the plates. It is very distinctive. I have a set of ten, but I always wanted twelve. I have looked for more of these plates but have never been able to find them.

When I opened up Ermon's cabinet, I instantly noticed he had the exact set of plates, and the sight of them caught me off guard. After I closed the door, I stepped back and tried to catch my breath. A woman entered the room and saw me staring at the cabinet.

"Are you okay?" she asked.

"I'm fine."

"What's in the cabinet?"

"Plates."

She opened the cabinet door and looked inside. "What a beautiful set of dishes," she said. As she closed the door she looked at me.

"You don't understand. Those are *my* plates." I knew this was no random coincidence. God was speaking to me, and I had to quiet my mind so I could hear His voice.

I told Ermon that story after we got to know each other. He laughs and tells people I only married him for those plates. He says I had the chance to complete my set and wasn't going to let it slip thorough my hands.

I couldn't get the sight of those plates out of my head. After a few months, I started asking my friends, "Tell me about Ermon Dyer."

Ermon and I may never have gotten together if it were not for a little cat God sent me. I thought I was progressing fine after Wayne died, but I really hadn't shed the tears I needed to. I had stayed strong and kept moving forward, but didn't allow myself to really mourn Wayne's passing. Wayne had died in January, and on July fourth, I was sitting on my patio when a little grey and white stray cat crawled up next to me.

I never had a pet as a child and never had been drawn to owning one. But there was something special about this animal, and I felt calm as he sat next to me. I eventually picked the cat up, and he nestled on the small of my neck. The tears flowed as I allowed myself to become attached to another living creature. It was the first time I felt close to anything or anyone after my second husband died.

That cat, I later named him Snow, became a big part of my healing process. After I became attached to Snow, I thought about the words in the Bible that teach us about "all creatures great and small." God uses everything, including animals, to help us heal. All we have to do is to be receptive to his love and grace.

Ermon was visiting my house one day when my mother was there. He saw how I picked up Snow and loved on him.

"I wish she would treat me like she treats that cat," he said to my mom.

After he left, Mother pulled me aside. "Little lady, I think you need to be careful." She could tell Ermon was interested in getting to know me.

When we first started dating, Ermon picked me up at the office, and we planned to spend the entire day together strolling through the antique stores in Guthrie, a quaint little town just north of Oklahoma City. Guthrie is one of those special places that have many old buildings, and as you drive through the main street you feel like you are going back in time. Several movies have been filmed there because it has a charm that cannot be recreated on a soundstage.

As Ermon and I were heading out, we were making small

talk and I mentioned I had seen this great sheepskin rug at the mall. It was beautiful and would fit with the southwest theme of my house.

On the way home, Ermon casually suggested we go to the mall. Once we were there, I told him I needed to go buy the rug. We got in the store, and he bought the rug for me.

He took the rug from the clerk and handed it to me. "Merry Christmas," he said.

I laughed and told him he only bought the rug to "seal the deal" so I would go out with him again. The rug sits underneath the coffee table in our living room, and everyone who comes over laughs and wants to know the story behind it. There is a story to it, and I love the chance to tell it and let people know how much Ermon loves me.

I knew what Ermon was up to. If he couldn't get me through the cat, he was going to get me through the rug.

When we got married in our church,. It was a beautiful day, and we shared that special moment with our friends and family. God gave us the gift of allowing my father and Ermon's mother to sign as witnesses on our wedding license. At our age, this was unheard of. I am so glad Daddy walked me down the aisle and placed my hand in Ermon's.

Ermon is a very secure man. He humbly accepts everything I bring into his life with little or no protest. He was in the Air Force for eight years, and then worked for the Federal Aviation Administration, and later at Tinker Air Force Base. He retired after more than thirty-five years. His work has taken him all over the world, but he would never tell you how accomplished he is. He is far too humble for that.

I am grateful Ermon is so secure. He has never felt threatened by my success or by the fact I honor my first two husbands. Many men would not have the confidence to allow their wives to talk about other men in their lives. But not my Ermon. He is strong and stable and I love him for it. Sometimes, when we have visitors over to the house, he will give them the grand tour and point out Wayne's artwork.

Ermon and I have the same work ethic, and we both have to stay busy. One of his favorite expressions is, "I'm gonna work until they carry me out."

I say it a little differently. I say, "I'm going to work until Jesus comes."

Even now, when he is at a stage in life when most people would be looking for ways to quietly fade into the background, Ermon is working. He has a heart for serving others and has a part-time job as an ambassador at a funeral home. Not only does he comfort families in their time of need, he enjoys working with the two young men who own the business. He takes great pride in watching them grow and treats them like grandsons.

I had never been around the funeral business, but Ermon has taught me so much about it, I now understand the great service they provide to others. We took my mother there one day, and it was comforting to see how relaxed she was. She isn't afraid of dying and looks forward to kneeling at the feet of our Heavenly Father when she is called home. We only live a few miles from the funeral home, and my mother decided she wanted them to handle her service when the time came.

"You don't think we live too far away from them, do you?" she asked me sweetly.

Another value Ermon and I share is our attitude toward death. I approach funerals with a sense of reverence and love, but I also try to add a dash of humor and fun. I think of Wayne and Roy now and feel uplifted. I don't linger on the pain like I did when it was fresh. Enduring the grieving process is like walking through a cemetery. At first, dirt as it is leveled out over the grave and it looks barren. As time passes, grass begins to grow, and you feel the grace of God soothing you. It becomes more reverent and joyful at the same time.

Humor is very healing spiritually, especially when we are able to laugh at ourselves. When you look in the mirror and don't take yourself too seriously, it changes your perspective and allows you to see things in a lighter mode.

Sometimes things get low at our office, and I try to find humor in the situation. If you look for humor, you can almost always find a solution to your problem. If you sit, cry, and only see the negative, you are not solving the problem.

We can find ourselves going through the same set of troubles over and over. Linda has a great visual for this. When that happens, she sees God with His hands on his hips. "You didn't get it that time, we are going to have to do it again," she imagines Him saying.

***The Look-A-Likes At Ermon's 75th Birthday And Reunion.
Cherie, Deen, Ermon, Butch And Kim.***

Reunion

I feel sorry for people who can't really laugh. Some people are so worried and uptight they can't let go. They miss so much of the wonderful journey of life.

Other people are so work oriented, it's hard for them to break loose and just enjoy being. They always have to be focused on work, and if they aren't, they feel guilty for taking time away from their careers. Work is important, but it's not as important as your family. I have learned to be in the now. I focus on what is in front of me. When it is time to work, I work. But when it is time to be with family, friends, or God, my sole focus is on that.

After Ermon moved into our neighborhood, Wayne managed

to volunteer him to be part of our neighborhood traffic committee. I didn't know it, but they got to know each other after Ermon walked past our house and saw one of Wayne's birdhouses we were using as a mailbox. Before long, Ermon was coming by to help Wayne with the birdhouses and churches he was making.

As we look back, we now know God moved Ermon to this neighborhood to care for me after Wayne had passed away. God also wanted him in my life to help care for mother after my father died.

When Ermon and I first started dating, I hesitated to tell him about my first two marriages. I wasn't sure how he would react. But he had the right to know these things, and I eventually told him how God had taken these two men before their time.

"You may want to rethink this relationship," I told him.

Ermon has a gift. He, like many men, does not express his feelings openly. But he has the ability to find cards that perfectly say what he is feeling. The cards always capture the moment and tell me what is on his mind. They have a depth and warmth beyond any cards I have ever seen. I don't know where he gets these cards. I'll let him keep that as his little secret. I just want him to keep giving me these wonderful little tokens of love.

Ermon is another person God brought into my life for a

reason. Neither of us knew it at the time, but as I was dealing with the challenges that had been placed before me, Ermon was walking on a separate path that was parallel to mine. We were going the same kind of pain at almost the same time.

Ermon has endured the pain of watching two relationships he cared about die. While he was stationed near the Panama Canal, he fell in love and married his first wife. They were blessed with two children, a boy and a girl. Unfortunately, her family did not approve of the relationship.

She returned to the Canal Zone to visit her family, and her father, a government official with powerful connections, used his influence to persuade his daughter to file for divorce. Ermon's wife later changed her name and the names of their children and went into hiding. Ermon had to face the shocking reality that his entire family had disappeared. He searched for years but wasn't able to find them. He was not able to watch his children grow up or to give them the love and support they needed.

He managed to bandage his wounded heart and tried loving again. Out of the blue, his second wife discovered her high school sweetheart was single and left Ermon after thirty-two years of marriage. Ermon was devastated, and I understood his pain. He had given his heart and soul to someone, but the relationship and people he cared so deeply for were taken from him.

Who would have known God would use such hurtful experiences to bring two people together? I was certain no one would ever understand what I had endured, and Ermon felt the same. Yet there is a common bond in the pain we have felt, had endured, and we have a powerful relationship today because of it.

Ermon is a very guarded man, and it is difficult for him to talk about how much when both of his marriages ended. No one should have to live through the pain and uncertainty of losing his family to death or the action of a spouse.

Ermon's story did not end there. Eventually, his children were able to locate him. They yearned for the love of their father and reached out to find him. The family was reunited in February of 1999, after being apart for forty-two years. Ermon is now able to enjoy the love and relationships he had been denied for so many years.

I had the pleasure of meeting his children before Ermon and I married. They made a special point to make me feel loved and involved. I could tell by how they treated their father they cherished him and felt a void because he had not been allowed to be there for them. Kim and Cherie, two of Ermon's daughters, told me how important it was to them that their father had found a lasting relationship that made him happy.

We had an engagement party at a local restaurant built to look like a castle. Ermon's daughters raised their glasses and offered us a toast. "Our father is non-returnable," they said. Isn't that a lovely sentiment? There is magic when people truly love others and want them to be happy and flourish, and we certainly felt it as Ermon's family paid tribute to him.

Ermon now has several grandchildren, and it is stunning to look at their pictures. They look so much like Ermon it is shocking. They all have the same, teeth, cheekbones, and noses.

Gayle And Ermon's Symbolic Rings.

Triangles

Like Roy and Wayne, Ermon has come to share my love for New Mexico. We enjoy traveling there whenever we have the chance. After we were married, we saw the most beautiful pair of gold and turquoise rings in a magazine. We took the picture with us to Santa Fe and found an amazing jeweler who recreated them. We wear them now as our wedding rings, and each time I see the gold lines zigzagging between the triangles of turquoise in Ermon's ring I am reminded of how blessed I am. It is fitting his ring has so many triangles on it. There are three equal lines of gold for the three golden men I have loved.

Another special place Ermon and I love is the beach. I first went to the ocean when I was eight years old. My family went to Seal Beach, California, and I remember standing on the shore as the waves crashed onto the sand. It was overwhelming to stand there and feel the presence of God. Roy and I took the girls to the beach at Houston, Texas, on a family trip. I went to Padre Island, Texas, as a retreat after Roy passed away. I stared out over the ocean and found comfort in looking at the end of the horizon, knowing I have so many special people waiting for me there.

The fourth time I visited the beach was with Ermon. He took me to Fort Lauderdale, Florida, and we visited his son. One of the most magical moments of my life happened when we went out under the moon and stars to watch turtles bury their eggs in the sand. I will never forget watching the mother turtles struggle to find dry land, and how they covered their eggs with sand before they retreated back to their home in the water. The sounds of the ocean were so different in the daytime than they were at night.

Ermon and I took a cruise shortly after we were married. We stood on deck at night and looked over the balcony. They only things we could see were the stars, and this helped us realize how we had no control over our lives. Only God can create such wonderful scenes, and He has the true power and control in our lives.

Connie Harris, one of my dear friends, says I am the only woman God has blessed with three very different husbands. She tells me she always thought Roy was very protective, Wayne was very outgoing, spontaneous and loved life, and Ermon is very protective. It is obvious he loves life and family passionately.

This year Ermon received a birthday card from Harvey, so he is now officially in the family. My daughters also gave him a father's day card and it has been a blessing to watch their relationship grow. It was hard for them to accept a new man in my life, and I can't blame them.

Much of the joy Ermon and I found may have to do with our age. As I have grown older, I appreciate the comfort and contentment that comes with aging. There is no pretention between us, and we both can look back on the roads we have travelled, and we have built confidence from all we have done and seen. This is a luxury the young cannot afford. When you are young and just starting out in life, your focus is on the future, and you are uncertain if you will achieve your goals and the desires of your heart. There is an excitement in the uncertainty and expectation of the journey. But when you have travelled further down the road and know your journey has been (and hopefully will continue to be) prosperous and joyful, you can relax and appreciate the view.

An Affair Of The Heart Founders.
Gayle, Lois, Anita, Susie, Eleanor, Linda And Connie.

An Affair of the Heart

As many of you know, the little craft show eight women created in their kitchens has grown beyond our wildest dreams. We now hold four shows in Oklahoma each year, two in Oklahoma City and two in Tulsa. Every year, thousands of women come out to see us and buy things for their homes.

Women are nest builders. They come to AAOTH to collect feathers, string, and so forth so they can build nests and provide warmth and shelter for their flocks. It is an honor so many people look forward to our shows. I have been told many times that some women plan entire weekends around coming to see us, and they are just as much a part of our extended family as the vendors I see each year.

Some ladies have a hard time explaining to their husbands how much AAOTH means to them. Here is the best way I have found to express it. It is the Super Bowl for women. It's an event we look forward to each year, and don't you dare try planning anything for me on that weekend.

In February of 2010, we celebrated the twenty-fifth anniversary of our show. We have garnered more awards and honors than I ever knew existed. There have been many kind words written about us in magazines and newspapers from places near and far. AAOTH was once reviewed in Sunshine Artist's magazine as one of the top twelve annual events.

There is a story I tell whenever I am fortunate to be asked to give a speech. This happened years ago, before debit cards were used. Our fall show is normally held on the last full weekend in October. One year there was a conflict at the fairgrounds, and we had to push it back a week. It never occurred to me this would be a problem.

The Monday after the show would normally have been held, I received a call from someone in the Federal Reserve. After he introduced himself, I wondered why he was calling me.

"What happened to An Affair of the Heart?" he asked.

"Nothing's happened. We're doing just fine."

"You didn't have it this year. Something must have happened."

I explained to him about our scheduling conflict. I then asked him why he had called me.

His answer surprised me. I had no idea our show had such an impact.

"Well, the Monday after AAOTH is the busiest Monday of the year for us. We have to hire additional people to process all the checks that come through. We were concerned when we didn't see all the checks this year." Who would have known our "kitchen table" business would have grown to the point the Federal Reserve would base hiring decisions on when we held our show?

My position in the company requires me to do much of the public relations work. Some people say I am the face and voice of AAOTH. It is a privilege to serve in any capacity that helps the company grow.

I have learned so much during the last twenty-five years I could get a job at the United Nations as a diplomat. As the business has grown, I have had to keep pace. The show is not just a check to me. I want the satisfaction of a job well done, knowing my efforts have made a positive difference for our customers, vendors, and the other ladies in the company.

During the show, I am constantly involved in conversations and problem solving. I spend a lot of time and energy being the "face" of the business, and I scurry from place to place. I'm not complaining. I love the business and the opportunities it has given me. But there are times I have to sneak to the bathroom to have a moment to myself.

When I come back, people will ask me where I was. I look them in the eyes. "I was giving my smile a rest."

I have been blessed in so many ways by working with the show, far too many to describe in one book. But the greatest gift it has brought me is friendship. I have become friends with some of the most loving, talented, creative, and special people God ever created. Many of these are our vendors, the people who come year after year to display their talents and sell the items they have created throughout the year.

Connie Harris   *Gayle Dyer*   *Linda Jeary*

Connie, Gayle & Linda.

Family

The show is not really a business. It is a family. We don't live together, and we are not related by blood, but we share a kindred spirit and are joined by God. We meet four times a year for family reunions, and we invite everyone else to browse and share in our joy.

We don't just deal with our vendors when it comes time to sign contracts. Our lives have intermingled, and we share in the joys and sorrows life brings us. Sometimes we will get a call at the office from one of our vendors and they will tell us they are sick or that someone close to them has died. They share with us, just like they would with their own family. I am proud they feel close enough to us to keep us informed of the milestones in their lives.

This reassures me we have built our business on Godly principles. If we were only concerned with profit and loss, we wouldn't have these special bonds. People know when you are treating them with true concern or if you have ulterior motives. We never want to be known as a company that cares more about money than people.

My friendship with Connie Harris began twenty-seven years ago, when she sold crafts out of Linda's store. Connie had a craft show in her home for many years. Several of us decided to start a bigger show. Connie was raising three kids and needed every penny she could earn from consignments.

In February of 1985, Connie, I, and six other women pooled $500 apiece and started the show. The next show was held a year later, in February of 1986. There we were, eight women who had just enough business experience to fill a thimble, but somehow we managed to get the show off the ground. To think back on how we started and how we have grown is a testament to the power of God.

Very few people gave us much of a chance when we started. "I don't know why you want to get into this," Connie's husband

John told her. "You will never make any money with eight partners." Her husband now proudly wears a badge at the show that displays the title, "Connie's husband." Once he saw it, Ermon had to have one and he now proudly wears it to every show.

It has been a blessing to watch Connie grow. She was timid when we first started the show, but she has finally come to understand her strengths and weaknesses. Like me, she is always working on polishing herself.

I know how fortunate I am to be part of such a successful business, but working with eight women has always been a challenge. This was especially true when we were starting and none of us had the experience to know if it would succeed or not. And the dynamics of working with other strong, capable, women have presented another difficulty. There were times when it seemed like none of us had our choo-choos on the same track. But God has put us together for a reason and in the place we should be. Whenever there are challenges in our lives, we should use these as learning opportunities and strive to be better people.

The show has turned into our livelihood, and into the livelihood of our vendors and the people who work at the show. I have developed a bond with many of them and care about them and their families. Our show has grown to be very well respected. The Oklahoma City shows are held on the state fairgrounds, and many of the people who work there have told us has a higher power is looking out for us.

They Serve And Protect.

Protection

We especially appreciate the police officers who work for us. They are a large part of why families feel safe coming out to our venue, and are the backbone of the show. Our officers are visible but not obtrusive.

They are the best of the best. We have an officer stationed inside every building to keep the vendor's wares safe. One year, we had a terrible rainstorm and one of the buildings leaked. Officers took turns mopping the floors and moving items throughout the night so they would not get damaged by the water. How many people would make this effort for complete strangers? They go above and beyond in every possible way.

The level of planning for any contingency is amazing. When you have as many people as we do converge for an event, you are bound to have some unexpected things happen. One of our customers had medical problems and was pronounced dead at the scene, but the emergency personnel were able to revive her. It turns out the woman was on a transplant list, but wouldn't miss the show despite her health problems. Another one of our shoppers had given blood before she attended the show and started to feel lightheaded. An ambulance was called, but she refused any help. She eventually signed a waiver so she could continue shopping. How many businesses can say they have that kind of loyalty?

We love the police officers who work at our shows, and we treat them like family. We have trams that bring people from the parking lot to the buildings. John, Connie's husband, made a sign one year so people would know where to stand for the tram to pick them up. It looked like a real traffic sign and the bottom of the pole was encased in cement. One day, we discovered that one of our officers had backed his car into one of our signs and bent it. We did a little investigating and discovered who the guilty party was. We used to feed our officers on the last day of the show, and that year we had cooked chili for them. We made a small, replica sign and bent it just like the real one was. As the guards filed in to eat, each one of them saw the little sign and who it was for. When the officer who had bent the sign came in and saw the miniature, he knew he had been found out. We all had a good laugh, the kind of laugh you can only share with people you truly love.

Others tell us when they come to our show it is like coming home. It is so nice to hear these things, and the words are validating. If you treat people like they need to be treated and don't yell or scream at them, they will bend over backwards to help you and to make sure people know how well you treated them.

At the end of each show, we try to do something special for all of our workers to tell them how much we appreciate their work. Connie makes pendants to give to them, and I try to write each of them a thank you note and personally thank them when each show ends.

The show is the most amazing business and has allowed me to make some of the most beautiful relationships. God has made it such a part of my life, sometimes I can't separate if from myself. It is our baby, and every show feels like we are giving birth to another bundle of joy.

I have been to enough shows and talked to enough vendors

to know at most shows likc ours, the owners or promoters are never there. We have taken a different approach. We want all of our vendors to see us and to feel they can talk to us like family. We want to know what we do well and what we need to improve. Taking complaints is an important part of any job and is one of the few ways you can really make sure your customers are satisfied. I wouldn't want to do business any other way.

Regardless of what you do in life, you have to let snide comments fly away. You cannot allow the hurtful words of someone else to keep you from achieving your goals. When someone says something hurtful they are really saying something about themselves. Confident, loving, sprit-filled people say loving and nurturing things. People who are wounded, angry, and feel unloved say spiteful and demeaning things. Don't take hateful words personally, but look at them as an opportunity to help someone in need.

Words are the hardest thing in the world to take back. Remember that when you think about saying words that might hurt someone. If you need to, carry a salt shaker with you and hold onto it during those times when your tongue might lead you to places you shouldn't go.

The show has taught me I am only responsible for myself.

I have no control over what others do or think. It is sometimes a struggle, but I have to remember to keep my emotions under control when others try to attack me.

I was blessed to have friends like Connie befriend my husbands, and they eventually came to love these men. Our husbands would play golf together, built a sign for show, and played cards at the show. Ermon also assists John with emergencies and crowd control.

Working with family presents a unique set of difficulties. When a family member reports to you, it changes the dynamic between the two of you. For this reason, we don't allow family members to work in the company offices. They can work for us on the weekends of the show, but they can't hold any management positions at the office.

When Connie's son was about eleven, he really wanted to work as my gopher. He wanted to be at the show and run whatever errands I needed. He was so committed to this he even wrote me a letter and said he didn't care if he was paid. I let him, and he did such a great job we hired him back the next year to work in one of our hospitality suites.

Linda And Gayle.

$2.50 Days

Another special friend is Linda Jeary. Linda and I met when we were children in school. We lived just six blocks from each other, across a busy street, and we were in Bluebirds together. I still have pictures of us when we were at the park on a merry-go-round. Our mothers were on the PTA together. My family moved across town when I started seventh grade, but we maintained our friendship off and on, even though we weren't able to see each other very often.

One day I visited the antique shop Linda and her parents owned. I wanted to talk to Bessie, Linda's mom, and Linda, because I was starting my own shop and wanted their advice. Once Linda and I saw each other, our friendship started right where we had left it.

Linda and I started a housekeeping business together, and we called it "Housekeeping with Heart." It wasn't a success by any means, but it kept us busy and off the streets. After work, we would sometimes go through the drive-in at Braum's. There were days we were so tired we couldn't count change, so we would just give the cashier two and a half dollars, which was barely enough to cover the cost of our orders. We called these, "two-fifty days."

After Roy passed away, God gave me a calling. It was to help lead Linda to the Lord. This was a blessing, not just to Linda, but to me as well. Teaching her about my joy in the Lord helped me heal. She and I have cried together, laughed together, and been angry together. We used to telephone each other and read scripture as encouragement. Together, we learned that there is no problem that can't be solved.

This is a very treasured relationship that has grown over the years without any effort. As Linda puts it, "Jesus joined us at the heart."

Our families became close as our friendship deepened. Wayne and Linda's mother both loved ice cream, and they would meet at the show and sneak off to get it. Wayne and I were at the hospital after Linda's mother had a stroke, and the two of them enjoyed their customary bowl.

Our friendship is strong because we have so much in common. Linda was also raised in a loving family. Her mother stayed home, and her father was a sweet, hard-working, and successful businessman.

She and I both enjoy working and believe we are doing the work God has given us. That's why the show has enjoyed success. She also understands God joined all of the owners of the show for His purpose

Linda has also enjoyed the growth of the show. She says it is like we have a tiger by the tail, and we don't want to let it go.

There is a special memory about Linda I have to share. Every year, Linda and I exchanged Christmas gifts. One year, she gave me a wonderfully wrapped bag. I didn't open it for several weeks. I was cleaning house on New Year's Day, putting away the Christmas presents, and opened Linda's gift. The bag was full of Hershey's kisses, but there was also a crystal heart inside. I set the heart on a table in my living room.

I had been praying for some time about what the new year would bring and was hoping God would reveal to me what I should do. As I looked at the heart Linda had given me, a ray of sunlight came through the window. The room was filled with a rainbow when the heart acted like a prism. I smiled, knowing it was God's promise to me that it was going to be a good year.

What keeps people going is having something to work for. God may take us in a different direction than we want to go, and this can give us more joy than we thought was possible.

If you look at it from a business perspective, the show makes no sense and shouldn't have survived. Eight women decided to create a one-day craft show. We had no business plan and no formal training. It just started and we followed. We worked ourselves silly handing out flyers and making PR calls.

When we started, we didn't even have furniture or an office. Our kitchen tables were our offices. No one knew what the show would become. But we knew God would provide everything as we needed it. We took every opportunity we could get without infringing on anybody else.

Only God could have made our business successful. We recognize this as a gift, and this keeps it together. Everyone in the group brought her own savor and spice to make a great soup.

Gayle.

Business
According to Gayle

AAOTH has given me many opportunities, and people sometimes ask me the secret to our success. I am fortunate to have learned many business lessons that have helped our company grow. I share them so you can use them in your life and in your organization.

Keep in mind many of these are not business lessons. They are life lessons. Your business will prosper only to the extent you apply these ideas in all facets of your life.

The most import reason we have a company that has grown

and prospered throughout the years is because our business is faith based. We believe we were put together by God for the purpose of creating a positive atmosphere and to improve the lives of families. We would not have succeeded without having faith in the Lord.

Along with faith, we have been obedient to God and His plan for us. We have listened to Him and followed Him, regardless of where He has asked us to go. Having faith is one thing. Being obedient and doing what He asks us to do is something else.

Respect is a very important part of any business. If you don't respect yourself, your partners, your employees, or your customers, you will not survive. Respect will come naturally when you build trust with those around you.

When your business succeeds, be humble. No one "does it by herself." If you start to have false pride, you will quickly be reminded of how much others have helped you. This may come from the words of those around you, or it may come when you look at your balance sheet and see how it is declining.

You must be patient with yourself and everyone in the company. Nothing happens overnight, and trying to force things to happen can hurt more than it helps. Think long-term and be willing to take time to see the results of your work.

A business is like a marriage. There will be good times, and there will be bad times. You have to make the decision to not get divorced. If you are truly committed to your business, you can work through the bad times and come through to the sunlight on the other side.

It is always important to think before you speak, especially in business dealings. Words are some of the most powerful things in the world. Kind words can turn a person's day around and help her build good thoughts and habits that transform her life. Hurtful, angry words can destroy her self-esteem and create negative thoughts that inhibit her ability to grow and achieve.

Some people take the attitude to "say it like it is." They believe they have the right to say whatever they want and if the people listening to them can't take it, it's just too bad. You can't make everybody happy, but you can consider the feelings of others

I don't take that approach. Why create conflict that can damage your relationships and limit your future business opportunities? Take a few extra minutes to select a few careful words and you can get more results.

When we started the show, we had to decide how we were going to handle things, and we often had meetings where things got a little more heated than they should have been. I prayed about this and God lead me to a wonderful solution.

At our next meeting, I placed a Bible and a salt shaker on the table. Some of the other women didn't know what to expect.

"We have to remember we are here because God brought us together," I said. "And we need to be sure all of our language is seasoned with salt just like He told us. If we don't put Him first, our business will never grow like it should."

Sometimes I still carry a salt shaker to remind myself to use kind constructive words, and not hurtful, divisive ones. I know what it feels like to have my ideas quashed by curt words, and I never want anyone to feel that way. I want people to walk away from me, even if we don't agree, feeling good about themselves and their abilities. In the long run, not only does this help other people, it helps me.

I hope you don't read this and think I am telling you to avoid conflict. Conflict is inevitable, and if you try to avoid it you will never be the person you can be. But there is a way to deal with conflict that allows you to preserve relationships. Don't burn bridges. You never know when you will need to find a way across the river.

And I will never be a doormat. For me, there is better way to resolving conflict than by striking out at others. You should value and cherish the relationships God has given you. Don't tear these down. Build them up.

I am amazed when I read stories of the trouble some companies have instilling business ethics in their employees and management. Ethics are not complicated. To be truly ethical, you need to put God first, others second, and yourself third. If you think in those terms, and take the action to carry it out, you will never face a dilemma you can't overcome. It is only when you place your needs above those of God or those around you that you start to have ethical challenges.

Learn to allow your ego go to the back. Don't worry about appearing to know everything or feeling like you have to have the right answers all of the time. It is not a do or die situation to get your own way.

You have to be a leader so that everybody wins. Being a leader doesn't always mean standing in the forefront with all the glory and praise. Sometimes a good leader has to step to the side and allow others to contribute in a meaningful way. A true leader often acts like a follower.

Focus on results, not credit. Let others shine when they come up with a great idea or are willing to go the extra mile.

There have been times I have made suggestions that were immediately rejected. It can hurt when this happens because I sometimes take it personally. But don't allow yourself to feel this way. It is amazing how often someone else will make the same suggestion at a later time and everyone is quick to praise and accept it. It is not important where the idea came from or who suggested it. What matters is that the work gets done and your business flourishes.

I try to be a cheerleader in our company. I tried to establish that mindset when we first started. I want everyone to succeed, feel good about themselves, and to understand what a valuable contribution they make to the company. No business would prosper unless all of the owners, managers, and employees do their jobs. Anyone who thinks they are the sole responsibility for any organization's success need to reconsider and reevaluate this.

I don't want to be the kind of person who grabs people by the ears and forces them forward. I want to be the kind of person who pulls and encourages people to be the people God meant them to be.

Some people tell me I am "self-made." I don't know if anyone is truly "self-made." Everyone has received an opportunity or encouragement from the people around him. Every honest businessman has had tremendous help along the way.

If someone does start to think he achieved something by himself, he needs to pay closer attention to who and what is around him. We constantly learn from those who are around us and the circumstances we face. I look back with humor at how little I knew about business and at how God provided for me and those around me. He always gave us the right thing at the right time.

Never forget to learn from those around you, and be mindful of the fact others will always be looking at you as a chance to learn. Everybody is an example. Some are just an example of what not to be. Everyone has something to teach you. Be humble and look to others so you can become a better person. It is not a sign of weakness to ask for help, and it does not make you a failure. Respecting the value that other people bring to the table will enrich your life and give you more joy than you imagined.

I suppose part of this attitude comes to me naturally. I have always been fascinated by the human mind. Psychology classes were always some of my favorite. I watch people and try to understand the fascinating mystery they present.

One Source.

Authority

I have always respected authority. I greatly admire people who have earned leadership positions by the sweat of their brows. Sometimes they disappoint us, but this shouldn't stop us from treating them with the respect they deserve. There are times when it is difficult to think positively about some people who are put in positions of power. Be respectful, even if all you can muster is respect for the office they hold.

It is also important for me to remember whatever my failures may be, I am forgiven. I am required to forgive others when they fall short of the mark. I have always prayed I will exhibit fruits of the Sprit, and that I am "Christ like" in all of my relationships.

Because I have developed a servant's attitude, I arise each

morning with a sense of joy. My cup is overflowing, and I am drinking from my saucer.

I treasure the people who have given freely to me. So many people have encouraged me, mentored me, lovingly corrected me, and given me their time with no expectation of receiving anything in return. These sweet gifts have allowed me to make my journey and have made it so much more colorful than it would have been otherwise.

One of my professors at the community college gave one of the nicest gifts I have ever received. She told me I was only the second person she had ever met who had a natural ability to be in public relations. I admired this woman so much because of her education and her words brought tears to my eyes.

I looked at the professor and told her, "I envy what you have in your mind." She said she respected my talents and skills and what I had been able to accomplish.

Part of the program at the community college paired students with mentors who were successful business leaders. I was assigned to the marketing representative who was in charge of the Children's Medical Research Center. She was very good at her job and it was a pleasure to be in a position to learn from her. CMRC was a non-profit organization, and I learned a lot about doing things for others.

Because of the success of our show, I was allowed to represent the owners when The Journal Record (the most respected business paper in the state) recognized fifty of the most respected businesswomen in Oklahoma. I was nominated three years in a row for this award, which is the maximum number of times you are allowed. The business is now represented in the paper's Hall of Fame.

Every year they would publish a short biography of all the winners. One of the years I attended I read the qualifications of the other nominees. All of the other women were well educated and their resumes were much more impressive than mine. I felt blessed to be in their company, and it was a very humbling experience. It was a miraculous event because I never felt I owned the credentials to be there.

"What am I doing here?" I thought during one of the presentations. "Only God can bring someone with such humble beginnings as mine to the same stage as these other people."

Remember that God is hammering you into a vessel. Pray that God will make you into a vessel worthy to help Him. This is a true servant's attitude.

Business is really about relationships. You can make your life and your business so much better by always striving to build positive relationships with those around you. One of the best business relationships I have built is with Kevin Duane. Kevin and I have known each other for years. He worked in the local media, and he helped us with our marketing. He and I have become close friends.

In fact, it took Wayne a little while to accept how close we were and to recognize he should not feel threatened by our friendship. I was truly honored when Kevin came to work for us full-time. He shares our vision and passion, and I know he will be a true asset to help take us to the next level.

Kevin will always hold a special place in my heart, and not just because of how much I admire and respect his professional abilities. When Kevin was married, he asked me to stand with him at the altar. I have never received any honor or award that even remotely compares to this. I would never have had such a privilege if Kevin and I had not believed that business is more than dollars and cents. It is about people.

I have another wonderful story about Kevin. When Wayne and I were making plans to get married, we decided that after the wedding we would live in my house. He decided to sell his furniture and some of his living room things. He ran an ad in the newspaper.

Kevin came and looked at the couch and thought about buying it. His sister was moving here from out-of-state and needed furniture. Wayne said he couldn't sell it to him. He was waiting to hear from someone moving from North Carolina who said she wanted to buy it. It turned out the woman was Kevin's sister. Isn't it amazing how God brings people together?

We send out many press packets to the media, government officials, and people involved in tourism. I try to make each one feel personal. I never want people to see something coming from me and think they are just a name on a list. I put a handwritten note in each one, but as the show has grown, this has become more and more difficult.

Always avoid debt, and run your business on a cash only basis. Debt will make you feel like a rat on a treadmill. You will waste all of your energy going round and round and at the end of the day you will have gone nowhere.

Material things in and of themselves will not make you happy. I like nice things, and I often splurge to get something nice for me or those close to me. But things really don't add any value to your life. Some people will never know what true contentment is. They struggle and struggle their entire lives to accumulate more and more things and never have the joy and peace being contentment brings.

Money should only be used as a measurement of the health of your organization. Your value is not measured by how much money you make. You are not more important than other people because you make more money than they do, and you are not valued any less if you make less money than others. Never confuse income or profit with character, obedience, or worth.

You can be a real sad mess if you don't look at things positively. Life wouldn't be any fun if you went through all of your days being sad. There is a great quote by Charles Swindoll that says this beautifully.

> The longer I live, the more I realize the impact of attitude on life. Attitude, to me, is more important than facts. It is more important than the past, than education, than money, than circumstances, than failures, than successes, than what other people think, say or do. It is more important than appearance, giftedness or skill. It will make or break a company... a church... a home. The remarkable thing is we have a choice every day regarding the attitude we embrace for that day. We cannot change our past... we cannot change the fact that people will act in a certain way. We cannot change the inevitable. The only thing we can do is play the one string we have, and that is our attitude... I am convinced that life is 10% what happens to me and 90% how I react to it.
>
> And so it is with you... we are in charge of our Attitudes.

Gayle And Ermon.

Farewell for Now

Thank you for taking the time to share my journey with me. I hope these words comforted and uplifted you. In some ways, my life has not been the easiest one.

But is has been one filled with unimaginable joy, nurturing relationships with loving friends and family, and more peace and grace than one woman could ask for. I've shed a few tears along the way, but I have also shared laughter, hugs, and validation with those I cherish and care about.

I hope that, if you take anything from the stories I have shared with you, you will remember when life seems the darkest and when everything you relied on comes crashing down, these can be times of amazing growth. Tragedies only stay tragedies if you choose to sit still and remain in place. If you look at them as a chance to draw closer to God, and take the courage to step through the door to the next part of your life, you will be taken to places with people you never would have dreamed of.

I am so blessed for the opportunities that have come my way throughout my life. I am even more blessed to have been surrounded by people who have loved me, mentored me, and given me the strength to rise above the challenges.

Pour yourself out in service to others. God will keep energizing you. You are a vessel for His purposes, and a vessel has to be empty before it can be filled again.

We only grow old if we stop loving. Never stop loving God, your neighbors, and yourself. You will have days when you think you are alone, lost, and don't want to take another step. When you feel that way, look out your window and watch the birds as they flit from tree to tree. Remember they carry no burdens and harbor no hate as they rejoice in what God has given them.

Don't be afraid to spread your wings and fly when storm clouds approach. Always remember to make your way to the birdbath after the clouds have gone, dip your toes in the water, and dance.

Desireé Y. Branson Eakle

Work has already begun on my next book to be released in 2011.

Please join me again for

Treasures of the Heart

Blessings,

Gayle